IMAGES

of America

LEVI STRAUSS & CO.

IMAGES
of America

LEVI STRAUSS
& CO.

Lynn Downey

ARCADIA
PUBLISHING

Copyright © 2007 by Lynn Downey
ISBN 978-1-5316-3522-0

Published by Arcadia Publishing
Charleston, South Carolina

Library of Congress Catalog Card Number: 2007927480

For all general information contact Arcadia Publishing at:
Telephone 843-853-2070
Fax 843-853-0044
E-mail sales@arcadiapublishing.com
For customer service and orders:
Toll-Free 1-888-313-2665

Visit us on the Internet at www.arcadiapublishing.com

To the men with picks and shovels who labored in mines by candlelight. To the cowboys of the prairie and the silver screen. To the dudes and dudines, the motorcycle rebels, and the ones who changed history in Berkeley and Berlin. To the generations around the world who have worn and loved their Levi's jeans, this book is dedicated.

CONTENTS

Acknowledgments   6

Introduction   7

1.   Open for Business   9

2.   The Blues Are Born   15

3.   A New Foundation   39

4.   A Western Icon   59

5.   The Denim Family   73

6.   Peace, Love, and Bell-Bottoms   91

7.   150 Years . . . and Counting   111

ACKNOWLEDGMENTS

Having the best job in the world means that I get to work with people who are professional, knowledgeable, and, even more important, fun. Many contributed to the safe passage of this volume from concept to bookshelf.

Archivist Stacia Fink, my partner in crime in the Levi Strauss & Co. Archives, kept our historical ship of state afloat so that I could concentrate on the book. Jeff Beckman was a stellar editor and cheerleader. Tom Onda, Jennifer Gunn, and Kris McInnes cheerfully tolerated my questions about legal and contractual issues. Jeanne Hangauer and Taina Kissinger of Visual Presentation did their usual digital magic and also provided original photography. Bob Chandler, my demented colleague at Wells Fargo, was a font of historical information, advice, and encouragement. John Poultney, editor extraordinaire, was a fun and patient guide through the entire process, from initial meeting to final celebratory lunch. Many thanks, John, for making sure I always had what I needed. Numerous other friends and colleagues contributed in myriad ways; you know who you are.

And a final thank you goes to Bob Haas for trusting me with his family's legacy.

INTRODUCTION

Several of the founding businesses of San Francisco still thrive in the "City by the Bay," and they have names that echo the unique needs of the city's Gold Rush settlers: Wells Fargo (banking), Ghirardelli (chocolate), and Boudin (sourdough bread), to name a few. And there's one more name known to consumers around the world—Levi Strauss & Co. (LS&CO.).

The eponymous company founded by Bavarian immigrant Levi Strauss in 1853 was first known for the fine dry goods it wholesaled to the small retailers of San Francisco and the Western states. Levi worked for his family's dry goods business in New York, called J. Strauss Brother & Co.; he and his brothers saw great opportunity in gold-fevered California, and Levi was chosen to undertake the trip and set up shop. In 1873, the company he founded revolutionized the clothing world by introducing the world's first blue jeans. More than 150 years later, LS&CO. is still at the forefront of jeanswear and casual-wear design and innovation.

Gold Rush San Francisco was a great place to be if person was in the dry goods business, and Levi Strauss was not the only entrepreneur to operate a warehouse on the city's waterfront. It was the perfect location from which to import and wholesale pants, coats, raincoats, scarves, garters, purses, blankets, collars, cuffs, handkerchiefs, or just about anything needed to make work and home life functional and comfortable. Dry goods wholesaling formed the bedrock of LS&CO.'s business for its first 20 years.

In 1873, Levi and Reno tailor Jacob Davis patented a new kind of extra-durable men's work pants—then called "waist overalls" or just "overalls," now called jeans. The denim pants were reinforced with copper rivets, perfectly suited to the needs of laboring men. A clothing factory was set up in San Francisco sometime after the patent was granted, though these details are sketchy thanks to the loss of the company's records in the 1906 earthquake and fire.

As the city and the West evolved, so did LS&CO.'s clothing offerings. Coats, jackets, and vests joined the expanding line of pants made of either cotton denim or a sturdy fabric called cotton duck. The clothes came in sizes for adults and children, though at this point, only for men and boys.

Levi was more than the sum of his wholesale inventory. He was committed to helping San Francisco prosper and equally committed to helping the less fortunate citizens of the city and its environs. In 1854, less than a year after starting his business, he made a donation to a local Protestant orphanage; in 1871, the company sent a healthy sum to the Chicago Fire Relief Fund; and in 1897, Levi provided funds to establish scholarships at the University of California, Berkeley. When he died in 1902, obituaries and books about San Francisco praised him as both an honorable businessman and a generous philanthropist.

His four nephews—Jacob, Sigmund, Louis, and Abraham Stern—carried on his business and his values and did not hesitate to rebuild the company after its total destruction in 1906. The Stern brothers introduced new products, including clothing for the active women of the West, children's playsuits, and fine khaki and corduroy trousers.

Sigmund Stern's son-in-law, Walter A. Haas, took over the company after Sigmund's death. He and his cousin, Daniel Koshland, transformed LS&CO. and kept it afloat despite the challenges of the Depression and World War II. Under their leadership, LS&CO. introduced women's jeans and fine sportswear and expanded distribution to include the high-end equestrian shops of New York. The company's links with the cowboy and the myth of the American West were cemented during this period, an association carried through from advertising to product design.

The 1950s through the early 1970s saw new leadership in the form of Walter Haas Jr. and his brother Peter Haas Sr. Distribution was expanded to the entire United States and then to Europe and Asia as new affiliates were opened. The company expanded beyond jeans and acquired a number of apparel-related firms in a bid to diversify its offerings. The Levi Strauss Foundation was created to coordinate the company's charitable programs, and new products aimed at the expanding suburban family and the burgeoning baby boom were introduced. The famous 501 jeans became the uniform of youth culture, and in 1971, LS&CO. went public for the first time in its history.

Transformation characterized the company and the fashion world as the 1980s began. LS&CO. divested itself of the subsidiaries acquired in the previous decade, went private with a record-setting leveraged buyout, and, with the introduction of the famous 501 Blues television campaign, ushered in a new fascination with the original blue jean. The business casual revolution was ignited with LS&CO.'s introduction of Dockers khakis in 1986. In addition, the company focused early on the growing threat of HIV/AIDS, creating policies and programs to educate its workforce and help infected employees around the world.

Today Levi Strauss & Co.—like its founder—is known equally for its quality clothing and its commitment to corporate citizenship.

One

OPEN FOR BUSINESS

In March 1853, the youngest member of the firm of J. Strauss Brother & Co. of New York City stepped off a steamship and onto one of San Francisco's many wharves. He was one of the city's newest entrepreneurs, the proprietor of the West Coast branch of the family business, but he gave this new enterprise his own name: Levi Strauss.

Born in Bavaria in 1829, Levi immigrated to New York with his mother and sisters around 1847. Brothers Louis and Jonas had a dry goods wholesaling business there, and Levi joined the family firm. By the early 1850s, the Gold Rush had turned San Francisco into a humming metropolis, and Levi was sent to California to represent J. Strauss Brother & Co. on the West Coast.

His first wholesale warehouse was on the north side of California Street between Sansome and Battery Streets. On May 7, 1853, the clipper ship *Oriental* arrived in the city from New York with his first shipment of dry goods, and six more ships arrived with merchandise for Levi before the year ended. The firm of "Levi Strauss" soon had retail customers throughout the West.

He did not build his business alone. Around 1856, his sister Fanny, her husband David Stern, and their son Jacob arrived in San Francisco from New York, and brother Louis joined the firm a year later. Levi moved his warehouse to a succession of larger quarters, and by 1864, he was living with Fanny and David's growing family. In 1866, the company moved to spacious headquarters at 14–16 Battery Street, and the corporate name was now "Levi Strauss & Co."

On February 11, 1872, the *San Francisco Chronicle* published an article about LS&CO. titled "Our Solid Merchants." It described in great detail the company's Battery Street headquarters, its wholesale inventory, offices, and the value of the stock on hand. The conclusion reveals how far Levi had come since 1853: "Every year is adding largely to the trade of the firm, and already the immense incomes place its members among the Merchant Princes of the Pacific Coast."

This is the house in Buttenheim, Bavaria, where Loeb Strauss was born, on February 26, 1829. He and a sister known as Fanny were the children of Hirsch Strauss and his second wife, Rebecca Haas. After Hirsch died in 1845, Rebecca, Loeb, Fanny, and possibly another sister known as Mary, made their way to New York, arriving around 1847. The older Strauss boys, Jonas and Louis, already had a dry goods wholesale business on the Lower East Side and young Loeb, now 18, started to learn the ropes. He also made a couple of important decisions: by 1850, he had changed his name to Levi (though it was spelled Levy on the 1850 census), and a year later he applied for American citizenship, getting his naturalization papers just a week before leaving New York for a new life in San Francisco in February 1853. Today the house where Levi was born is a museum dedicated to his life and his jeans, managed by the city of Buttenheim.

A young Levi Strauss strikes a serious pose in this 1860s photograph. How he got his firm underway after his arrival is still a mystery, though it is likely he had the names of important contacts and potential customers when he landed. He prospered early; in a list of assessments of personal property in the August 20, 1857, issue of the *San Francisco Evening Bulletin*, his worth was given as $20,000, equal to about $400,000 today. It was not all smooth sailing though. Less than a month after this article appeared, the company lost $76,441.79 worth of "treasure" (probably gold being shipped back to the family in New York) when the steamship *Central America* was wrecked in a hurricane and sunk off Charleston on September 12. This was not a disaster for the company, though; four years later Levi shipped nearly $50,000 in "treasure" to New York. With his brother-in-law David Stern and older brother Louis now part of the firm, he had help to expand his business and his customer base.

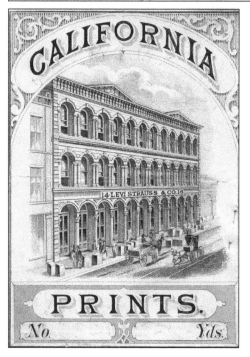

Hardie and Kennedy, of Foresthill, California, was among the first of Levi's dry goods customers, one of the few whose invoices still exist and that date to the company's early years. As this billhead shows, Levi had quite a selection of merchandise available: men's and women's hose or stockings, checked shirts, and side stripe "cass" pants ("cassimere" is a medium weight wool used for men's clothing). A variety of clothing was obviously important for this retailer's customers, who were located in the foothills northeast of Sacramento.

This booklet from around 1873 (the LS&CO. Archives only has the cover and a partial page in its collection) was probably a swatch book of fabrics printed in California and available from LS&CO. The front features a fine engraving of the company's Battery Street headquarters, and an inside page claims that the goods are "warranted in all respects perfectly fast Colors. The cloths are uniform and equal in manufacture to any goods produced in this country."

Colman & Morris · Volcano

1869 Dec 29	To Balance	654 73	1870 Feby 4	By Cash	130 95

Oul Raphael · Stockton

1869 Dec 29	To Balance	392	1870 Feby 28	By Cash (a/c)	274 41
1874 Jany 31	do	267			

Tong Hop · Honolulu

1869 Dec 29	To Balance	1268 87			

A. Jacobs · North Bloomfield

1869 Dec 29	To Balance	562 28	Jany 19	By Cash 3 2	281 13

This ledger page from 1869 shows the geographic range of Levi's business: from Volcano and North Bloomfield, Gold Rush towns in California's western Sierras, to Honolulu, Hawai`i, then under the rule of King Kamehameha V.

In 1866, Levi Strauss & Co. moved to spacious new headquarters at 14–16 Battery Street, at the southeast corner of Battery and Pine. The *San Francisco Morning Call* described Levi's office there in an 1892 article: "The chief of one of the largest wholesale importing and manufacturing firms on the coast is Levi Strauss, an old-timer and well known man in the downtown district. His office is at the rear end of the lower floor of his big warehouse, and to reach it you have to walk past big stacks of dry goods. . . . Inside you find everything is very plain, and not the least attempt at decoration is visible. It is just a business office, plain and simple, fitted up for 'strictly business' only."

Two

THE BLUES ARE BORN

The blue jean—that most American of products—came out of a collaboration between two immigrants: Levi Strauss and Latvian native Jacob Davis, a tailor living in Reno, Nevada.

In January 1871, the wife of a local laborer asked Jacob to make a pair of sturdy pants for her husband. Using a heavy white fabric called cotton duck, Jacob fashioned the trousers as usual. He wanted to make the pants last longer, so he used a few metal rivets to fasten the pockets and presented the finished product to his customer, who paid him $3. Within a few months, Jacob was making so many pairs he decided to patent the process and look for a business partner to help him mass-produce the pants.

Enter Levi Strauss, his fabric supplier. Jacob wrote to Levi sometime in 1872, and in July of that year, the two men applied for a patent on the new invention. Their correspondence was lost in 1906, so it is not known what kind of agreement they forged, but what is known is the important thing: on May 20, 1873, the U.S. Patent and Trademark Office granted Levi Strauss & Co. and Jacob Davis patent No. 139,121 for an "Improvement in Fastening Pocket-Openings" on men's work pants: the first blue jeans.

Jacob moved his family to San Francisco and was put in charge of LS&CO.'s first manufacturing venture. The partners decided to make the riveted waist overalls out of blue denim, the traditional fabric for workwear; they also used brown cotton duck. These trousers, along with other garments such as coats and vests, were added to LS&CO.'s massive wholesale dry goods inventory and to the products carried by the company's sales force.

Levi continued at the helm of LS&CO. for the next 30 years. He incorporated the company in 1890, bringing in his four nephews—Jacob, Sigmund, Louis, and Abraham Stern—as shareholders. He devoted time and money to causes and institutions he felt strongly about, and he was a fixture among the businessmen of San Francisco. He died in September 1902, and the Stern brothers inherited their uncle's thriving business. The earthquake and fire of 1906 destroyed LS&CO.'s warehouses and factory, but the firm was up and running again in short order, ready for a new city in a new century.

Born in Riga, Latvia, in 1831, Jacob Davis immigrated to the U.S. in 1854. By 1856, he was in San Francisco and kept on moving around the West, marrying in 1865. Four years later, he settled into tailoring in a shop at 31 Virginia Street in Reno, Nevada. There he made his first pair of riveted trousers and from there wrote to Levi Strauss about patenting this new process.

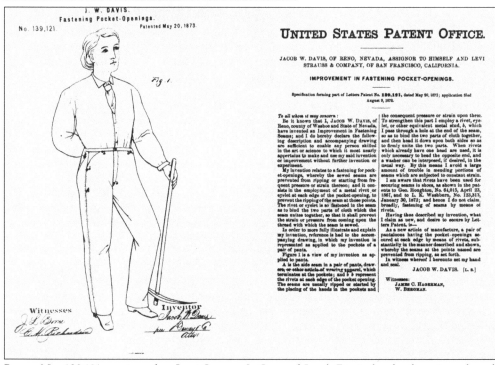

Patent No. 139,121 was issued to Levi Strauss & Co. and Jacob Davis for the first riveted work pants, known today as blue jeans. Sometime before his death in 1908, Davis sold his interest in the patent back to LS&CO. Today his descendants run Ben Davis Company.

As early as 1879—and possibly earlier—the copper rivets on the waist overalls were stamped with the company's initials and the patent date. The pants were called waist overalls or, more commonly, "overalls" until the 1960s, when the more modern term "jeans" was first used. If one wanted bib overalls, one had to ask for those specifically. (Photograph by Hangauer/Kissinger.)

The Levi Strauss & Co. Archives owns the oldest pair of jeans in the world: this pair from c. 1879. These are the famous 501 jeans, known between 1873 and 1890 as "XX"—a term that was also the designation for the denim used in their manufacture, which came from the Amoskeag Mill in Manchester, New Hampshire. The pants have the Arcuate stitching design on the single back pocket (the second back pocket was added in 1901). They also have the traditional watch pocket in the front. (Photograph by Hangauer/Kissinger.)

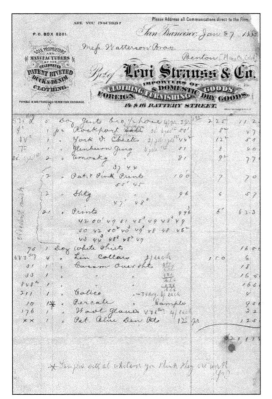

The XX was sometimes called Patented Blue Denim Pants, as seen on this, the earliest retailer invoice in the LS&CO. Archives that shows the sale of the company's flagship product. Benton, now known as Benton Hot Springs, was a mining town in Mono County, California.

Levi and Jacob took care to protect their invention, even making sure they maintained their rights as patent holders in the United Kingdom in 1874. To make the concept very clear, they included illustrations of a pair of pants, a vest, and an intricate hunting coat, similar to one now held by the LS&CO. Archives.

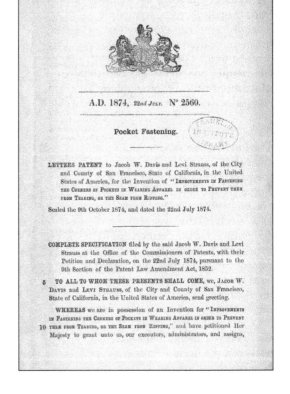

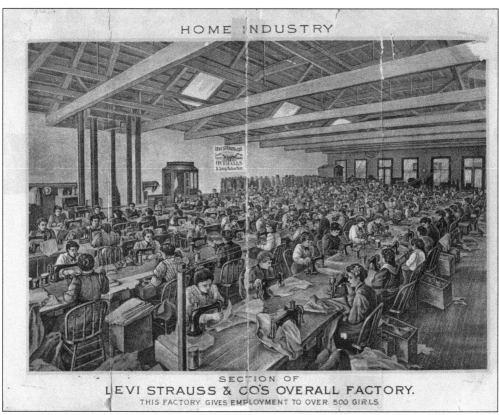

HOME INDUSTRY

SECTION OF
LEVI STRAUSS & CO'S OVERALL FACTORY.
THIS FACTORY GIVES EMPLOYMENT TO OVER 500 GIRLS

Oral tradition states that the riveted pants and other workwear products were initially sewn by women working in their homes. How the riveting was done, however, is unknown. But Levi Strauss & Co. had full-scale manufacturing in San Francisco by the late 1880s at 32½ Fremont Street, south of Market.

LS&CO. made a variety of riveted products within a very few years after receiving the patent. Among them were these denim pants, known today as the "Nevada Jeans," which were named for the state where this vintage pair was found in the 1990s. Acquired by LS&CO. in 2001 for $46,532, this 1880s pair has a special pocket on the left thigh for a folding ruler. (Photograph by Hangauer/Kissinger.)

Miners, such as this pair from California, were among the first users of the new riveted waist overalls.

Spring Bottom Pants were probably added to the line in the late 1880s. Although they were also considered workwear—since they were manufactured with the copper rivets—they were designed to be worn by men such as factory superintendents or bookkeepers. "Spring Bottom" meant the pants had a flare to the leg opening.

LS&CO. created the Two Horse trademark in 1886, placing it on a leather patch that was used on pants, heavy shirts, and coats. Before 1886, the leather patch had the company's name and phrases about the strength of the riveted products. This logo was probably created because the patent was due to expire in 1890; the Two Horse symbolized the strength of the original riveted clothing in the face of future competition.

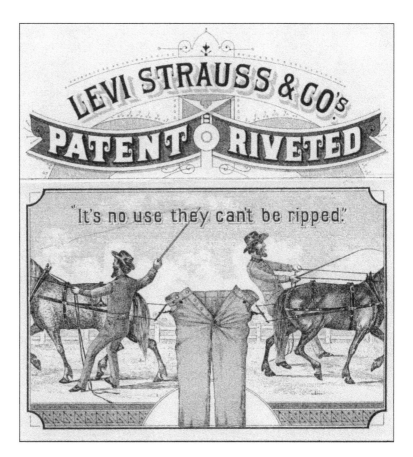

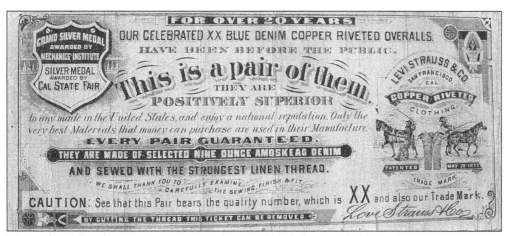

This is the earliest known "Guarantee Ticket," a label made of oilcloth, which was first sewn onto the back pocket of the jeans around 1892. Prior to 1892, the wording on the ticket about fabric, fit, etc. was printed on the interior pocket bag. After the patent expired in 1890, the company decided to print this information on something that could be seen when the pants were on the shelf of the local mercantile. (Courtesy Hitoshi Yamada.)

In 1960, LS&CO. received a letter from Henry Lash, who recounted his father's memories from 1888: "My grandfather had a lace and embroidery firm and used to send my Dad in to the [LS&CO.] office . . . Dad was . . . terribly impressed with seeing the great Mr. Levi Strauss himself, San Francisco's famous & outstanding manufacturer; what impressed Dad most was that everybody in the office called him Levi. . . . 'I still remember Levi Strauss as one of the finest, kindest, and friendliest gentlemen I've ever met.'"

By the 1890s, Levi Strauss had firmly established himself as a local philanthropist. In 1896, he helped pay for electric light in the library of the University of California, Berkeley. The following year, he established scholarships for students at the university. In the 1900 *Blue and Gold* yearbook, Levi shares a page with Phoebe Hearst and other Berkeley benefactors. In 1898, the first recipients of the Levi Strauss Scholarship—nearly half of whom were women—presented him with an resolution expressing their gratitude.

OUR BENEFACTORS

Levi had four nephews, the sons of his sister Fanny, and all were associated with the company. Jacob Stern (right, 1851–1924) was the oldest of Levi Strauss's nephews and became president of the company upon his uncle's death in 1902. Sigmund Stern (below, 1857–1928) was the company vice president and succeeded Jacob at the helm of Levi Strauss & Co. when his brother died in 1924. Brother Louis Stern was the company's representative in New York, and both he and his brother Abraham died while Jacob was head of the firm. Under the two older Stern brothers, the company introduced new and innovative products and participated in the 1915 Panama-Pacific International Exposition.

This lithostone, or early printing plate, was used by a local printer to make the oilcloth Guarantee Ticket, which was sewn onto the back pocket of the Spring Bottom Pants. This printer had other interesting clients as well, such as Old Deacon whiskey and Italian Swiss Colony wines and brandies.

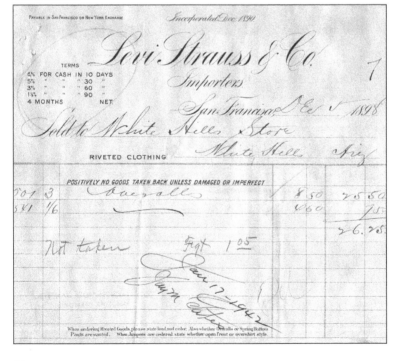

By 1890, when the patent expired, LS&CO. was making such a variety of riveted garments that it was decided to give each one a unique three-digit lot number. The number 501 was given to the original riveted blue denim jean. Why this number was chosen remains unknown, but any of Levi's riveted products whose lot number began with the number "5" was considered of the highest quality.

LS&CO. offered its retailers small printed items to give to their customers as gifts with purchase, with room for the store name and location. The reverse side of this little gem is an 1899 calendar.

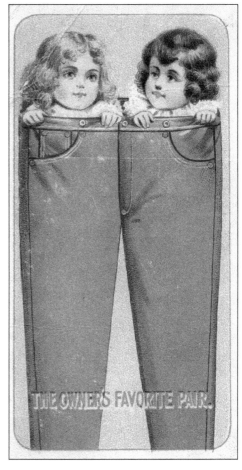

San Francisco boasted many newspapers and broadsheets for residents who didn't speak English. LS&CO. put these to good use for its advertising, such as this German-language item from 1893.

This late 1890s handbill tells a lot. The company was eager to portray the strength of the riveted pants in a compelling way, and Levi Strauss must have had a sense of humor: that is his face going over the fence. This image also graced the back cover of a pamphlet of children's stories in 1897 called "Bonny Birds."

Trade cards were a 19th-century form of business cards, but they were also considered a collectible. LS&CO. printed up a series of trade cards showing miners, engineers, and other consumers wearing the famous riveted clothing. These were given to store owners who then gave them to their customers when they bought a pair of Levi's overalls or other garments. Many people pasted the cards into scrapbooks or traded them, much like baseball and other cards today.

Handbills were used to illustrate and describe the company's line of riveted goods before it released its first retailer catalog in 1900. This 1899 item shows not only the varied product line but also the many kinds of people who wore the garments.

This is the reverse side of the 1899 handbill, used to describe the important selling points of the riveted trousers, "blouses" (jackets), and "jumpers" (heavyweight shirts).

The company placed display advertisements for the riveted trousers in newspapers all over the West. This advertisement appeared in the *Bodie Miner-Index* in 1898. Newspapers aimed at miners were particularly useful for spreading the word about the overalls, and Bodie, California, was one of the most well-known (or notorious) mining towns in the West.

Northern California mining communities also had their share of newsprint, and LS&CO. placed advertisements in papers such as the *Tuolumne Herald*. This advertisement was one of a sophisticated series of images, which ran in 1900 and 1902.

Levi Strauss & Co. employees have gathered for company picnics and parties for over 100 years. This get-together took place on Angel Island, near Marin County in San Francisco Bay, on Washington's birthday in 1899.

Sports tournaments have also been an LS&CO. tradition since the 19th century. This medal commemorates the company baseball team's victory over rival dry goods house Murphy, Grant and Company on September 9, 1886. (Photograph by Hangauer/Kissinger.)

Fairs and trade shows were an important way for LS&CO. to show off the riveted pants and other garments. The location for this 1898 trade shown is unknown, but the display of clothing and advertising is an important clue to understanding what the company was producing before 1906.

San Francisco's Mechanics' Institute was established in 1854 to serve the educational needs of the city's exploding Gold Rush population. It established a reading room, lecture series, and manufacturers' fairs to help promote local industry. Levi Strauss & Co. won a number of medals at these fairs for its riveted clothing and for the wool produced at the Marysville Woolen Mill, one of two mills owned by LS&CO. (The other was the Mission and Pacific Woolen Mills, formerly owned by William Ralston.)

Salesman Joe Frank had a spectacularly long career with Levi Strauss & Co. He was born in Baker, Oregon, in 1876 and was hired in July 1896 as an order clerk—while Levi Strauss himself was still alive and still actively involved with the company. Three years later, he was a traveling salesman with a territory that ranged from San Francisco to Oregon, but his main focus was in the area around Sacramento and the gold country. He delivered products via horse-drawn wagon and once took a tram across the American River to make a delivery. In 1949, when he was 73, he returned to San Francisco to work in the home office training new salesmen. The company celebrated his 70th anniversary in July 1966, and he retired in 1968 after 72 years on the job. He died in January 1977 at the age of 100.

Along with miners, cowboys were among the first customers for the riveted clothing. These cowpunchers are working their trade in Texas in 1902, and within a few years, real cowboys would be wearing their Levi's jeans as extras in the first Western films of the silent-movie era.

LS&CO.'s clothing was also popular among California's agricultural workers. This group poses in Elk Grove, near Sacramento, around 1900.

As the 20th century and his seventh decade approached, Levi Strauss brought his nephews into the business, incorporating LS&CO. as a California corporation in 1890. But he never gave up the reins, presiding as chairman of the first board meeting and continuing to endorse company checks.

Levi Strauss died at the home of nephew Jacob Stern on September 26, 1902, at age 73. On the day of his funeral, the company shut down so employees could attend the services. Rabbi Jacob Voorsanger of Temple Emanu-El gave the eulogy, and Levi was buried at Home of Peace Cemetery in Colma. The four Stern brothers—Jacob, Sigmund, Abraham, and Louis—inherited their uncle's business. Their sisters received large cash legacies, and Levi's will also benefited many local charities.

33

Levi Strauss & Co. printed full-length retailer catalogs beginning in 1900. The front pages featured the line of riveted products, with the rest of the catalog devoted to the huge selection of dry goods the company distributed. The covers of the first catalogs had simple drawings of the headquarters and warehouse, but by 1904, the company hired artists to create evocative and eye-catching front and back cover artwork. Salesmen gave these to the stores in their territory, replacing the one-page handbills of the 19th century.

LS&CO. devoted the inside covers of its own catalogs to full-page advertising, such as this page from c. 1904. "For Men Who Toil" was a popular slogan, and in this advertisement, the company is poking fun at its own image as a manufacturer of tough workwear for tough workingmen.

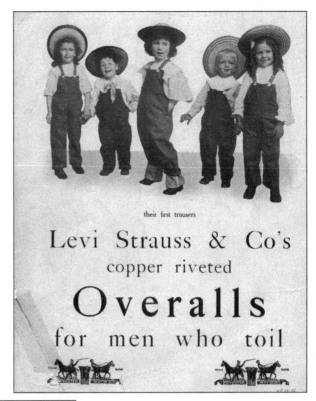

The dry goods pages of LS&CO.'s catalogs were always attractively designed, and each item was described in enough detail to help the retailer make the best choices for his store inventory. This page from 1905 shows off a selection of women's fine purses and handbags.

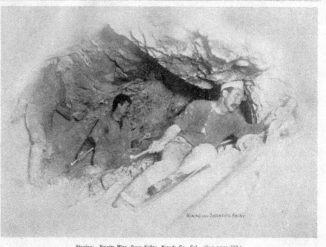

MINING
AND
SCIENTIFIC PRESS.
AND PACIFIC ELECTRICAL REVIEW.

No. 2090.—VOLUME LXXXI. Number 6. SAN FRANCISCO, SATURDAY, AUGUST 11, 1900. THREE DOLLARS PER ANNUM. Single Copies, Ten Cents.

Testing Oils.

A good way to test oils is to place them side by side on blotting paper, and place this for a short time on the cylinder chest or on a steam heater. The oil which penetrates the blotting paper quickest and spreads widest over it is always the poorest oil; the oil which spreads widest in part and leaves a defined ring in the center, must be a compounded oil, as it shows by its lightness and quicker disappearance of the outer ring that it is compounded from material of a very light gravity. If on longer exposure to heat, or by giving it more time, the whole of the oil on the blotting paper disappears, the sample must be composed entirely of mineral oil; and when an inner ring with a well-discernible ridge is formed and remains longer, a proportion of paraffine-holding stock must have been compounded with a lighter mineral oil; and when a center ring of decided outline and darker color is formed, and no permanent translucency imparted to the paper, the compound must have been made of light hydrocarbon oil with an addition of still residuum stock, however well defined or bleached.

THE highest voltage used for electrical transmission outside of California is in the Provo plant of the Telluride Power Transmission Co. in Utah, which

Stoping: Empire Mine, Grass Valley, Nevada Co., Cal. (See page 152.)

Miners got the fine illustration treatment on the inside cover of a Levi's catalog from c. 1905 (left). Note the similarity between the drawing of the miner and the photograph on the cover of the August 11, 1900, issue of *Mining and Scientific Press* (above). Miners and men in associated industries were likely very familiar with this photograph. And since they were wearing Levi's riveted overalls, LS&CO. felt it would be useful to create an illustration that would both advertise the products and make a connection to these consumers via an image that was also not copyrighted.

LS&CO. still had its baseball team in the early 20th century. Named "Elesco"—a phonetic rendering of the company's initials—the team members came from all parts of the company, from the basement to the sales floor. This photograph dates to around 1913.

Gifts with purchase have always been popular with consumers. This little wallet from c. 1900 was made of brown cotton duck, the same fabric used on some of the riveted pants and outerwear. Designed to hold a fishing license, it featured the company's Two Horse logo.

The earthquake of April 18, 1906, did little or no damage to LS&CO.'s headquarters on Battery Street, but the building was in the path of the fire, which roared through the financial district later that day. Quick thinking employees threw ledgers into a vault before fleeing the fire, the only company assets which survived the event. When it was safe to return, employees took shifts guarding the vault until it cooled completely, to prevent the spontaneous combustion of the contents when it was opened.

The Stern brothers put this advertisement in the April 27 edition of the *San Francisco Chronicle* to let customers and employees know that the company was "positively" resuming business. Employees were advised that they were still on the payroll, and those who wished to resume their jobs were asked to register at the factory on Clay Street in Oakland where the company made its line of "Sunset" label shirts.

Three

A New Foundation

Levi Strauss taught his nephews well. Despite losing everything the company owned in the disaster of 1906, the Stern brothers quickly secured temporary offices in San Francisco and Oakland and began construction on new headquarters, a warehouse, and a factory located on Valencia Street in San Francisco.

They also poured new life into the company's clothing offerings and advertising. Levi and Jacob had expanded the product line beyond the riveted garments to include a selection of both dress and work shirts. The Sterns now offered women's clothing, dressy men's khaki pants, and innovative children's playsuits to their retail customers, supporting the new products with creative advertising at the Panama-Pacific International Exposition, in movie theaters, via brochures, and on billboards.

The denim for the jeans and other riveted clothing had originally come from the Amoskeag Mill in Manchester, New Hampshire. At the turn of the 20th century, Amoskeag was the largest textile producer in the world, but during and after World War I its fortunes waned, due to competition from southern mills and a flurry of labor unrest. In 1915, LS&CO. searched around for a new denim supplier and began to purchase fabric from Cone Mills in Greensboro, North Carolina. By 1922, the company sourced all of its fabric from Cone, which in turn created the famous "red selvage" denim specifically for 501 jeans.

Sigmund Stern's son-in-law Walter A. Haas joined the business in 1919, and three years later Walter brought in his cousin Daniel Koshland to work with him. In 1926, the men went to the factory on Valencia Street and handed out bonus checks to factory workers; possibly one of the first such instances in the garment industry. Walter Haas took over the business upon Sigmund's death in 1928, and he and Daniel Koshland worked in tandem for the next 30 years.

As the decade ended and the perils of the 1930s were still unknown, the company made one of its most important business decisions since first making jeans: it registered the name Levi's as a trademark.

As LS&CO. planned its rebirth after the disaster of 1906, the factory work was transferred to a building at Tenth and Clay Streets in Oakland. The line of "Sunset" label dress and work shirts had been made at this location since around 1901. Here employees registered for work and potential employees for the new factory were interviewed.

A large vacant lot on San Francisco's Valencia Street between Brosnan and Clinton Park Streets was chosen to be the site of LS&CO.'s new factory. Designed by Albert Pissis, the architect most famous for the Flood Building at Powell and Market Streets, the building went up quickly, opening in November 1906.

Construction of the new headquarters and dry goods showroom at the northeast corner of Battery and Pine Streets took a bit longer. Until the building's completion in 1908, LS&CO. ran the business for awhile from Abraham Stern's house on Pacific Avenue, then from a building at Sixth and South Streets (today's Daggett Street).

The company was proud of its modern new building, now at 98 Battery Street. It was featured on the covers of company catalogs from 1911 until 1929.

Before putting the company headquarters on the cover of its retailer catalogs, LS&CO. renewed its tradition of using fine seasonal illustrations. The art nouveau movement was clearly an influence in these post-earthquake catalogs.

One final art nouveau flourish graced the cover of the 1908–1909 catalog.

The Two Horse trademark was important to LS&CO. After 1900, the company registered and therefore protected it against copying in Australia, South Africa, and Japan. This is the Japanese trademark document, which dates to 1908.

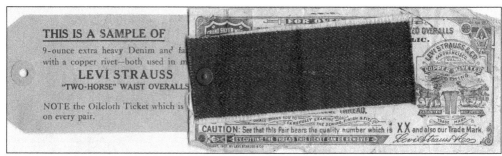

In order to convince potential retailers that they should carry the Levi's riveted denim overalls in their stores—instead of the growing number of competitors' products—salesmen gave them samples of the denim and the oilcloth Guarantee Ticket held together with the famous copper rivet.

OFFICE OF

LEVI STRAUSS & CO.

San Francisco, Cal., ___4/7___ 191_4_

Dear Sir:

Our representative, **MR. J. W. YOCUM** will have the pleasure

of calling on you on or about ___Apr 17/8___

with his complete line.

Very truly yours,

Levi Strauss & Co.

Salesmen had vast territories to cover, and they had competition from companies that were now making their own riveted denim products. J. W. Yocum was in charge of the territory around San Jose, California.

Denim was the foundation of LS&CO.'s line of manufactured clothing, but the company understood that not all workingmen were laborers. Men who worked in offices and as factory supervisors needed high-quality clothing too, and to meet this need, the company began offering fine khaki and corduroy pants, vests, and coats around 1905.

Levi Strauss & Co. was a big supporter of the Panama-Pacific International Exposition of 1915. As early as 1912, LS&CO. printed the PPIE logo on the back of its catalogs to help promote the upcoming fair to its retail customers.

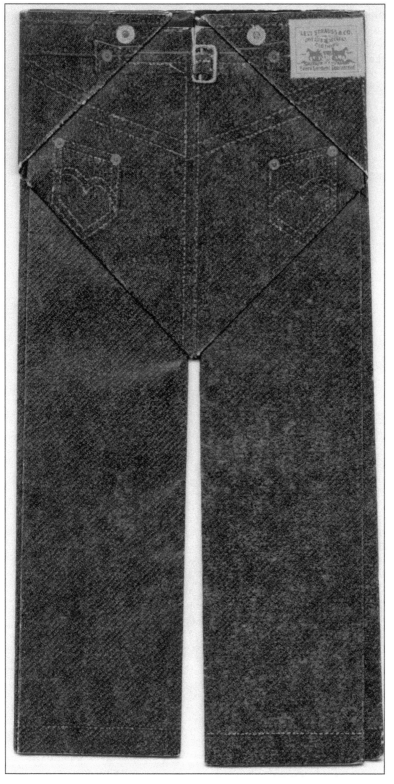

The Levi Strauss & Co. booth at the PPIE had a small sewing line in the Palace of Manufactures, where visitors could see how the children's garment "Koveralls" were made. Koveralls one-piece denim playsuits were first created in 1912, with bright red accents and gold-colored buttons on the drop seat. It was a popular product by the time the fair opened, so the company put many advertising dollars behind its promotion. LS&CO. held special Koveralls events for children throughout the run of the fair and handed out commemorative pins to visitors. The company also created this intricately folded brochure, which was handed out at the booth. It was 7.5 inches high, 3.5 inches wide, and made out of heavy paper in the shape of a pair of the overalls, complete with stitching and rivets.

When the PPIE brochure was unfolded, it opened up into a single vertical sheet, 22 inches high by 7 inches wide. Full color illustrations of the array of LS&CO. products covered the entire side: Koveralls and Koverall Nighties and overalls and bib overalls for men and boys, all in a variety of fabrics. There was also a drawing of the factory booth at the PPIE and prominent displays of the Two Horse trademark.

In 1917, a hard rock miner named Homer Campbell bought a pair of Levi's overalls at Brayton's Commercial Company in Wickenburg, Arizona. In 1920, he sent them back to LS&CO. because they had not held up as well as the other Levi's he had worn. Actually, what didn't hold up was the denim padding he sewed all over the jeans; the pants themselves were still intact underneath. This pair was recreated in 2003 as the "Celebration Jean" to commemorate the company's 150th anniversary. (Photograph by Hangauer/Kissinger.)

Levi Strauss & Co. understood early that women needed clothing to allow them freedom of movement for activities unique to the West. In 1918, LS&CO. created Freedom-Alls, designed for both housework and play, made in sailcloth and lightweight cotton. A one-piece tunic over balloon pants, Freedom-Alls were patented in April 1918, a year after the United States entered World War I, its name evocative not only of personal freedom but of the liberty language of the day.

In 1914, Sigmund Stern's daughter Elise married San Francisco native Walter A. Haas (1889–1979). In 1919, Stern asked his son-in-law to come into the business, and he gave him a very specific mission: turn the sagging business around in two years. He succeeded, and after becoming president in 1928, Walter brought the company into a period of modernization that prepared it for the challenges of the 20th century. He implemented a cost-accounting system, spent an unprecedented $25,000 on outdoor advertising at the start of the Depression, and cemented the links between the brand and the American West while expanding sales across the United States and into Europe after World War II.

Daniel Koshland (1892–1979) was Walter Haas's cousin, and in 1922, Koshland joined him at LS&CO. He served as vice president, treasurer, and president from 1955 to 1958. Dan had a deep commitment to social reform and worked with many city agencies to support causes such as education for disabled children. Dan and Walter worked together for over 30 years, each bringing a head for business and a compassionate heart to the helm of LS&CO.

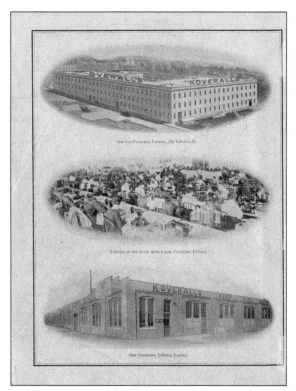

The Koveralls were so popular that a new factory in Frankfort, Indiana, was opened in 1920 to manage the production of the playsuit, and then the company's complete line of children's wear. The factory closed in 1940, and Koveralls and most of the other non-denim children's clothing was phased out around 1942.

This 1920s photograph of L. F. Protzman, LS&CO.'s sales representative in Fairbanks, Alaska, was proudly labeled, "Farthest North Sample Room." Alaska was still wild territory in the early 20th century, though men had worn Levi's overalls in the area since the Klondike gold rush of 1897. Other salesmen included I. L. Fletcher in Phoenix, J. H. Shaw in Portland, and E. J. Waterman in Honolulu.

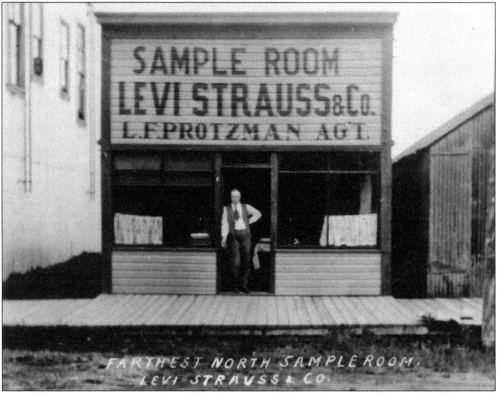

Although the company was printing full catalogs of the riveted clothing and the wholesale dry goods, LS&CO. sometimes printed up special flyers about work clothing for its retailers. Store owners could also print their name and location on the flyers and give them to customers to entice them to buy more Levi's products.

Bib overalls were a small but important business for LS&CO., and they were aimed at very specific professions: engineers, oil workers, and farmers, to name a few. Bib or engineer overalls had attributes that were important to emphasize in advertising: for example, elastic suspenders for ease of movement and a pocket for a folding ruler with a special "guard" so it wouldn't fall out and get lost.

After Freedom-Alls, the next big thing in women's clothing from LS&CO. was hiking togs, in finely woven khaki, introduced in the early 1920s. As with Freedom-Alls, the "outing" wear was designed for women who had active lives and needed sturdy, yet feminine clothing. Knickerbockers, which buttoned at the knee; blouses; coats; and hats could be mixed and matched depending on the activity or the weather. Women had finally won the vote in 1920, and with the Jazz Age waiting in the wings, Western women took the wheel, took to the air, and took to the national parks. The LS&CO. Archives has two pairs of the knickerbockers and the outing coat in its collections.

Levi Strauss & Co. management and, especially, the sales force understood that not every customer spoke English as his first language. As the company distributed its products throughout the 11 Western states and even into the Pacific Rim, flyers and handbills were printed up in Spanish, Portuguese, and Chinese and handed out in locales where the languages were spoken. These flyers date to the mid-1920s, and others from the same period feature well-known cowboys wearing the Levi's overalls. The flyers were also printed in English, so that the message about the overalls and the bib overalls was consistent across languages and cultures.

Free Moving Picture Slides

The illustrations show a new series of eight Moving Picture Slides. The names of firms will be inserted in the space after the words "For Sale By." The slides are beautifully hand colored, showing the garments in their actual colors and will be sent Free on request. Order slides by Nos.

LEVI STRAUSS & CO.
98 Battery St., San Francisco

Slide No. 1.   Waist Overalls

Slide No. 2.   Waist and Bib Overalls

Slide No. 3.   Bib Overalls

Slide No. 4.   Home Run Blouses and Shirts

Slide No. 5.   Home Run Shirts and Blouses

Slide No. 6.   Home Run Covert Family

Slide No. 7.   Koveralls and Playsuits

Slide No. 8.   Koveralls

Every automobile owner, every chauffeur and every man who works around an automobile should have one. Patent drop seat. No buttons to scratch the machine. Plenty of pockets. Dust protectors in the sleeve. Made in Blue Denim and in Light Weight Brown Duck.

A Wonderful Garment

Price $22.00 per doz. net

Retail selling price printed on every garment

$2.50 the Suit

Sold in following sizes only—crotch measurements:

Size	1	2	3	4	5	6	7	8	9
Trunk	58	60	62	64	66	68	70	72	74

Remove the coat, then measure from the center of the right shoulder, down the front, through the crotch, and on up back to center of right shoulder, the starting point

Levi Strauss & Co.
San Francisco, Cal.

KOVER-UPS
(Patents Pending)

Are manufactured by Levi Strauss & Co. San Francisco, and are sold to the dealer upon the condition that they shall not be sold or offered for sale for less than $2.50 the suit.

REMOVE THE ELASTIC BEFORE SENDING THE GARMENT TO THE LAUNDRY.

LS&CO. has always kept abreast of what was happening in popular culture. In the 1920s, movie theaters projected slides with advertisements for local businesses before the movie started or in between double features. To make use of this unique marketing opportunity, the company created a series of "Moving Picture Slides" for various products in the late 1920s. They were designed so that store owners could print their names on the slides, each featuring a photograph of one of Levi's garments.

The rise of the automobile did not get past LS&CO. either. In the early 1920s, the Koverup was created, a denim coverall designed for anyone who had a car in his or her life.

By the mid-1920s, LS&CO. management started to see an interesting trend: any pair of riveted denim pants was called "Levi's"—no matter whom the manufacturer was. While it was flattering to have the company's name stand for all denim products, it was alarming from a business point of view. Becoming the generic for a consumer product diluted the power of the original, so in 1927, the company applied for a new trademark: the name "Levi's." The Guarantee Ticket was redesigned that year so that instead of reading "This Is A Pair Of Them," as seen on the original from 1892, the new ticket read, "This Is A Pair Of Levi's." The trademark was registered in 1928, and to this day, the company staunchly defends the name against all potential infringers.

Besides flyers, catalogs, movie picture slides, and gifts with purchase, LS&CO. spread the word about its products through painted signage all over the West. Before the billboard came along, there was the painted barn, roof, store signboard, and bare brick wall, all surfaces used at one time by LS&CO. beginning in the 1920s. Many of the signs were in California—Alturas, Fort Bidwell, Susanville, Woodland, Sonoma, Napa, and Redlands. Beyond the Golden State, there were signs in Caldwell and Hailey, Idaho; Jacksonville, Oregon; and Eureka, Utah. Pictured here are Lordsburg, New Mexico ("Sandstorm in Lordsburg" is written on the back of the photograph), and a men's mercantile in Sacramento at Third and L Streets, both in the 1920s or early 1930s.

Newspapers were always an important venue for advertising, both for the company and its retailers. These "ad mats" were given to store owners to make it easy for them to place an advertisement in their local newspaper. They could choose the style that suited their budget or their product mix, whether overalls or bib overalls. The 1927 ad mat is an important one; it shows the use of "Levi's" the same year the company applied to register the word as a trademark.

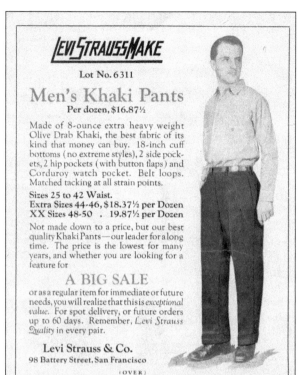

Khaki pants were still part of the product mix in the late 1920s. Here they are still dressy wear, even though the LS&CO. Archives has a few pairs from this era that were found in either caves or mines. This meant that someone's fine khakis were torn or stained and were then used as workwear until they became completely unwearable.

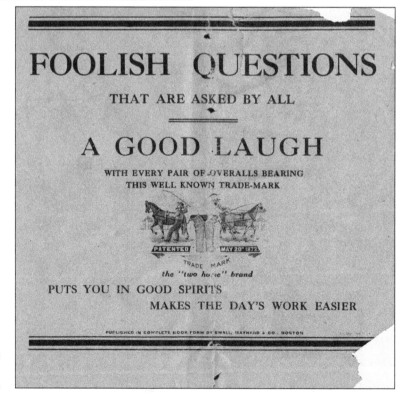

Gifts with purchase in the 1920s included this little booklet of cartoons and jokes.

Four

A WESTERN ICON

Business decisions in the 1930s ranged from countering competition, to managing the effects of the Depression, to choosing an image to represent the famous jeans.

When the patent for riveted clothing passed into the public domain in 1890, an influx of competitors entered the marketplace. Products with names such as Sweet-Orr, Boss of the Road, Can't Bust 'Em, The Boss, and Non-Pareil (made by baseball and dry goods rival Murphy, Grant) fought with LS&CO. for customers and market share. To meet this challenge, LS&CO. decided to focus its advertising energies on a unifying image that best represented the individual products and the company's western roots: the cowboy. At the same time, the cowboy's flip side—the dude—was also getting some of the company's attention.

The dude ranch was a very popular destination for Easterners lured by the romance of the West and the myth of the American cowboy. The company jumped onto this trend with its first line of Western wear in the mid-1930s. LS&CO.'s first jean for women also made an appearance at this time, designed specifically for leisure.

Western themes were appropriate for LS&CO. because, with the exception of places such as Best and Company and Kaufman's in New York City, which carried the dude ranch clothing, the firm was only selling its products in the Western states. When the World's Fair came to San Francisco in 1939, LS&CO. had a major presence, designing a mechanical rodeo to entertain visitors and expose the popular products to audiences from beyond the West.

Product innovation also flourished during the Depression years and into the years of World War II. The famous red Tab came around in 1936 and the back pocket rivets on the jeans were covered in 1937. Changes to the jeans were mandated by the U.S. government during the war, and in-store advertising demonstrated the company's commitment to the war effort. LS&CO. continued its groundbreaking tradition of commitment to social justice as well, opening racially integrated factories throughout Northern California.

After the war was over, LS&CO. looked at the popularity of its products and decided to expand distribution to the entire United States and, by the end of the 1950s, even beyond U.S. borders.

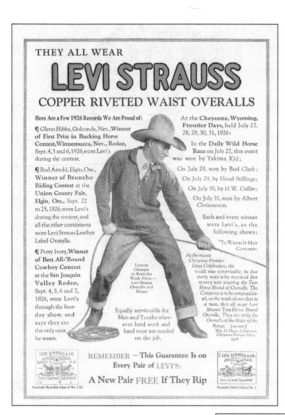

As LS&CO. moved into the 1930s, the company began to link itself to the cowboy in advertising and promotions. With competition coming from other Western brands, LS&CO. decided to choose an icon to represent its brand and its products. The cowboy was a figure whose popularity gained strength in both literature and film as the 20th century progressed. Cowboys were also early and loyal consumers, so it made sense to choose this image from among the dozens of other workingmen who wore the riveted overalls.

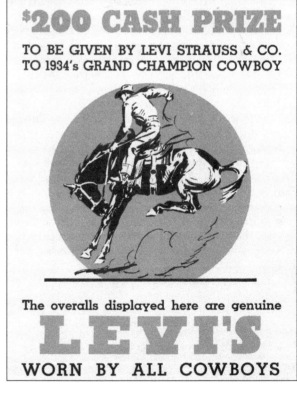

In response to the dude ranch craze of the 1930s—where real cattle ranches gave cowboy vacations to non-Western types—LS&CO. created its first sportswear line: Dude Ranch Duds. Dudes (men) and dudines (women) who had never worn denim in their lives were now buying Levi's jeans, jackets, and other clothing to wear while horseback riding and singing by the campfire.

One of the most popular items in the Dude Ranch Duds line was the Rodeo Shirt, made of heavy rayon satin described as "soft as the afterglow of a Western sunset." The colors ranged from white, black, and gold to wine, winter rose, and royal blue.

No. 701

Lady Levi's, the company's first jean for women, was launched in 1934 and was soon part of the Dude Ranch Duds line. They were "tailored to fit and look neat and trim on the feminine figure" and were considered dude ranch or sportswear, not workwear. The few western women who ran their own cattle ranches wore the men's overalls instead.

Vogue magazine ran an article about dude ranching in their summer travel issue of May 15, 1935. The article was illustrated with a drawing of two stylish women in Lady Levi's along with a caption that stated, "True Western chic was invented by cowboys, and the moment you veer from their tenets, you are lost." LS&CO. used the drawing and caption in this mailer, which was sent to all retailers soon after the magazine appeared.

WHAT! OVERALLS IN VOGUE?

ON THE OPPOSITE PAGE: "LEVI'S" . . . THE FAMOUS COWBOYS'
OVERALLS, AS SKETCHED BY VOGUE IN
BEST & CO.'S DUDE RANCH DEPARTMENT

"LEVI'S" is the Far Western cowboys' name for a particular sort of tailored "blue jeans" that they've been wearing for some 70 years; it's short for "Levi Strauss Copper-Riveted Waist Overalls." If you're a reader of western novels and stories, or of Will Rogers' writings, you've doubtless seen many references to LEVI'S.

A cowboy without LEVI'S—just isn't a cowboy. Naturally, since they are so much in evidence at the dude ranches, the guests have adopted them.

And so you have the newest outdoor vogue for women —LEVI'S—worn by the knowing, not merely on dude ranches, but at the more exclusive resorts, beaches, and camps, throughout the country.

HOW LEVI'S GOT THAT WAY

The slim-legged, low-waisted lines that women rave about in LEVI'S are not mere styling. They are made that way to give perfect comfort in the saddle. But they are equally comfortable, as well as smart, for walking, motoring, or just loafing.

The hand-applied copper rivets are not a mere embellishment, but have a history and a real utility. LEVI'S have been made with these copper rivets for 72 years, as a reinforcement at the pockets and other points of strain.

Until very recently, LEVI'S were made only for men. Women had to take them that way, or leave them. Now LEVI'S are also specially made for women. The cut has been modified just sufficiently to conform to feminine lines without destroying its distinctiveness, and the denim has been processed so that it is soft and comfortable. They are guaranteed not to shrink or rip.

SHOPS ALL OVER THE COUNTRY, which pride themselves on being in the forefront of style, are stocking and displaying LEVI'S. You may still stock yours for the summer season. Using the order blank below will bring you prompt delivery from our Frankfort, Indiana plant. Fill in the sizes required or have us send you an assortment of the most popular sizes.

ORDER BLANK
MAIL TO

LEVI STRAUSS & CO. SAN FRANCISCO, CALIF.
Please ship by (express) (freight) _____ dozen LEVI'S for women, style 701, at $16.50 per doz.*

Waist									Length					
31	24	25	26	27	28	29	30	31	32	33	34	36		
32														
33														
34														

*Our regular terms are 1 per cent, 10 days: net 60. Any other desired terms may be arranged by means of a comparable adjustment in the price.

LEVI STRAUSS & CO.

SAN FRANCISCO · FRANKFORT, INDIANA · LOS ANGELES
· · · NEW YORK OFFICE · 40 WORTH STREET · · ·

WHAT THE WELL DRESSED YOUNGSTER WILL WEAR IN 1932

LEVI STRAUSS & CO. ❖ PRICE LIST

LS&CO. has offered children's clothing since the end of the 19th century. In the early 1930s, the company created an array of playwear that began with Koveralls and continued with the California Sun garment, a summertime cotton item whose design and style invoked the sunny paradise that California represented. Also available was a line of khaki garments under the Home Run label, which featured a little baseball diamond. Home Run was where some of the most creative clothing resided, including a baseball uniform and a junior aviator outfit made as an homage to Charles Lindbergh.

CALIFORNIA SUN GARMENTS FOR GIRLS

Lot		Ages	Price per Doz.
352	Green, blue and red small flower design.	1/8	$7.50
354	Blue, green and brown flower design.	1/8	7.50
		9/12	9.00

FRUIT OF THE LOOM FABRICS. Beach overalls, long flare legs, contrasting colored bib, button on shoulders with bow, and reversible hat to match.

314	White bib, royal blue pants, red insert; blue and white hat.	1/8	7.50
315	White bib, red pants, blue insert; red and white hat.	1/8	7.50
		9/12	9.00

FRUIT OF THE LOOM FABRICS. Beach pajama suit, sleeveless, double breasted effect upper, flare leg pants and hat to match.

319	Blue, rose and green blazer stripe design, white belt and piping with stripe hat.	1/8	10.50
321	Blue, green and red modernistic plaid design, matched belt and piping with hat to match.	1/8	10.50
		9/12	12.00

FRUIT OF THE LOOM FABRICS. Beach ensemble, sleeveless upper buttoning on shoulder, with long flare leg pants, separate sleeveless bolero jacket and poke bonnet to match.

317	Blue, gold and red polka dot design; pants and bonnet; plain color bolero jacket.	1/8	10.50
318	Red, green and blue candy stripe design; pants and bonnet; matched plain color bolero jacket.	1/8	10.50
		9/12	12.00

THE DAWN OF BETTER TIMES

"After the darkness comes the dawn"... On every hand we see evidence of the dawn of better times... We are glad, not only for ourselves, but for our thousands of loyal dealers throughout the West... We firmly believe that you, as well as ourselves, will now enjoy steadily improving conditions finally resulting in a return of normal and sound prosperity.

But we will not be content to *wait* for better times... we plan to *work* for better times... That is why we take both pride and pleasure in announcing the immediate start of a heavy advertising schedule for

LEVI STRAUSS
OVERALLS

Broadsides were elaborate brochures given to retailers to let them know what kind of advertising LS&CO. would be doing in the coming year. When the Depression hit America, it also hit LS&CO. and its retail customers, and the company used the broadside/mailer as a way to reassure store owners about the future of the business. The broadside for 1933 echoed Franklin Delano Roosevelt's sense of optimism in its opening pages, which heralded "the dawn" of prosperous times.

By 1936, many clothing companies were making dark blue denim overalls with copper rivets and a waistband patch, and this made it difficult for company management to distinguish Levi's products from the competition at rodeos, parades, or other events. So sales manager Chris Lucier created, in that same year, the famous red Tab with the word LEVI'S stitched in white in all capital letters. It was sewn onto the left side of the right back pocket and then trademarked to protect both the Tab and the brand name. Red was chosen because it contrasted well with the dark blue denim and was easy to see. (Photograph by Hangauer/Kissinger.)

Among the many items available to use as in-store advertising was a 3-foot-tall wooden cowboy torso with 9-foot-long denim legs ending in a pair of wooden boots. Designed to be displayed from either side, the back of the cowboy pointed out LS&CO.'s newest trademark to all store visitors.

In 1937, LS&CO. made a change to the construction of the back pockets in response to complaints from consumers. Although everyone loved the strength of the rivets, they tended to scratch furniture and saddles, so the back pockets were sewn over the rivets, to solve this problem. In 1966, the rivets were removed completely and replaced with heavy stitching, as they eventually wore through even the toughest denim.

Consumers were used to seeing the rivets in the back pockets of their Levi's overalls, so when they were covered up in 1937, the company devised the pocket "flasher," which was inserted into the right back pocket before the pants were shipped to the company's retailers. The flasher assured consumers that the rivets were "still there."

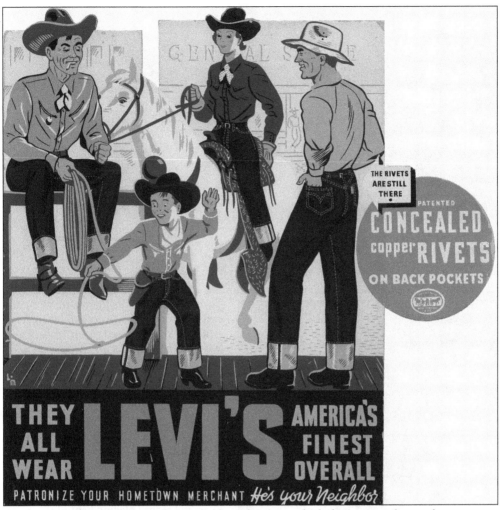

As the 1930s progressed, cowboys—both authentic and "dudes"—were featured on in-store advertising, on flyers, and in display advertising. Second only to cowboys in company advertising were workingmen, as seen in the bottom image, which shows cowpunchers sharing the spotlight with a miner, a lumberjack, and a farmer.

LEVI'S ELECTRIC RODEO — THE TALK OF TREASURE ISLAND

READ THE INSIDE STORY
of LEVI'S ELECTRIC RODEO

LEVI'S *Guide* TO TREASURE ISLAND
THE 1939 GOLDEN GATE INTERNATIONAL EXPOSITION

**LEVI'S OVERALLS
ON THE JOB
HELPING BUILD
THE WORLD'S FAIR**

**LEVI'S EXHIBIT
In Vacationland**
Moves and Talks

See the World's Only Miniature Rodeo

"It moves. It talks. Its figures are all hand-carved likenesses of famous rodeo people. And they're all dressed in authentic Western togs." So begins the text on a 1939 postcard created by LS&CO. to celebrate the Levi's Mechanical Rodeo, made for the Golden Gate International Exposition of 1939, held on man-made Treasure Island in San Francisco Bay. LS&CO. set up its puppets in Vacationland, and they were dressed in miniature Levi's overalls, satin rodeo shirts, and cowboy hats. They sat on the fence and sang cowboy songs (thanks to a vinyl record playing behind the display), and the revolving stage allowed mechanical animals to show up to entertain the crowd as well. In addition to the postcard, LS&CO. made up a special brochure showing how the rodeo was made, and both were given to visitors. After the fair closed, the puppets were put on a truck and sent around to help with war-bond drives during World War II.

A popular gift with purchase beginning in the 1930s was the check blotter, used in the era of fountain pens; wet ink remained on paper after the pen was used and blotting paper was applied to blot or soak up the ink so it would not smear. LS&CO. printed advertising images on heavy blotting paper, along with the name and city of the Levi's retailer, who received a supply for the store. When a consumer bought a Levi's product, he or she received a blotter as a thank you.

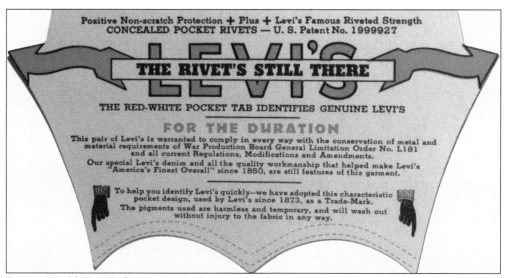

During World War II, the rationing of raw materials meant some changes had to be made to the riveted overalls. Rivets were removed from the watch pocket and the base of the button fly; no one really liked that one anyway as it tended to heat up when the wearer was crouched in front of a campfire (and unlike the watch pocket, the "crotch" rivet was not replaced when the war was over). In addition, the U.S. government said that the famous Arcuate stitching—the double arches on the back pockets—had to be removed, as the threaded design was decorative only and had no function. In order to preserve the design, sewing machine workers painted the Arcuate on the back pockets of the overalls. The company also created a new pocket flasher to explain the change, saying that "For the Duration" of the war, consumers would see painted stitching only. (Photograph of Arcuate by Hangauer/Kissinger.)

Advertising during the war still had a Western flair, but some of the in-store pieces, called "counter cards" as they were placed on counters where Levi's products were sold, took on imagery and wording that reflected wartime, especially with these two examples. In "Food Fights for Freedom," a Levi's-wearing cowboy herds cattle that will eventually feed soldiers overseas, and in "When There's Work to Be Done," a stevedore moves a box, which will move the country to victory. All counter cards exhorted consumers to "Buy War Bonds."

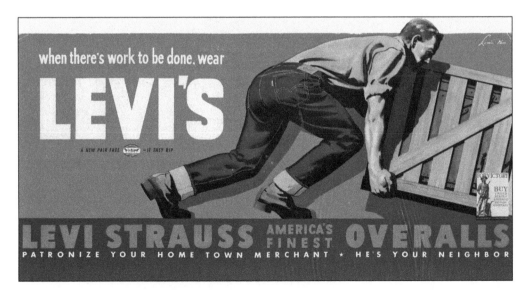

LS&CO. opened more factories in California during the 1940s, and in contrast to the practices in many other businesses and even the U.S. military, these facilities were racially integrated. This is a shot of the factory in Vallejo, California, in the mid-1940s.

TELEPHONE GARFIELD 6200

LEVI STRAUSS & COMPANY
MANUFACTURERS AND DISTRIBUTORS

PINE AND BATTERY STREETS

CHARLES C. HAPPHOLDT   SAN FRANCISCO

The dry goods wholesaling, begun by Levi Strauss in 1853 and which had worked in tandem with the company's own clothing manufacture, was discontinued after World War II so the firm could concentrate on making its own apparel, a side of the business that continued to thrive. This is one of the last business cards that reflected both sides of the warehouse.

Five

THE DENIM FAMILY

LS&CO. shared in the prosperity of postwar America and saw the importance of the nuclear family to American business. Early in the 1950s, collections of denim and cotton sportswear called Denim Family and Lighter Blues made their appearance at LS&CO. retailers. Western-themed clothing was still strong, and so was the image of the cowboy in company advertising. However, the family and the family teenager began to appear more and more in print and in-store marketing efforts. America revered the suburban lifestyle of television programs such as *Leave It to Beaver* and *Father Knows Best*, and the popularity of jeans was occasionally incorporated into the series' plotlines.

Even as jeans gained in popularity and gained new consumers, they also took on a new personality, thanks both to culture and to Hollywood. Many high schools banned jeans on campus because they were too casual or, even worse, an expression of rebellion. Films such as *The Wild One* put antiestablishment rebels and lawbreakers in jeans and on motorcycles, and *Rebel Without a Cause* cemented the link between juvenile delinquency and denim. These efforts were a reaction to a powerful strain of nonconformity in 1950s America, seen in everything from Beat culture to painting and poetry. In 1959, an outraged New Jersey mother wrote to LS&CO. complaining about an advertisement for jeans, which said they were "Right for School." In a letter dated August 29, 1957, she wrote, "While I have to admit that this may be 'right for school' in San Francisco, in the west, or in some rural areas I can assure that it is in bad taste and '<u>not right for School</u>' in the East."

As the business thrived, the company formed the Levi Strauss Foundation to coordinate its charitable efforts. And thanks to American soldiers taking their Levi's jeans with them overseas, a new wave of interest in the products arose in both Europe and Asia.

Daniel Koshland served as company president in from 1955 to 1958, and he was succeeded by Walter Haas Jr., who would preside over a period of astonishing growth during a time of even greater cultural turmoil.

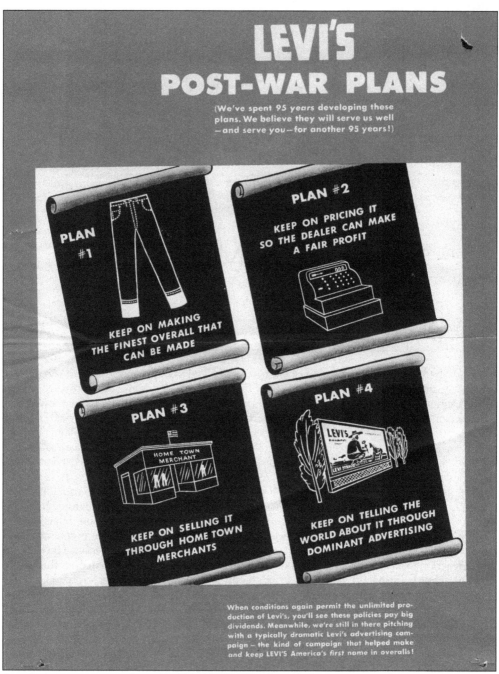

Broadsides given to retailers after World War II reflected the optimism of a victorious nation. The country, and its shopkeepers, had to build themselves back up, and LS&CO. was ready to help with strong advertising and efforts to get production back up to speed.

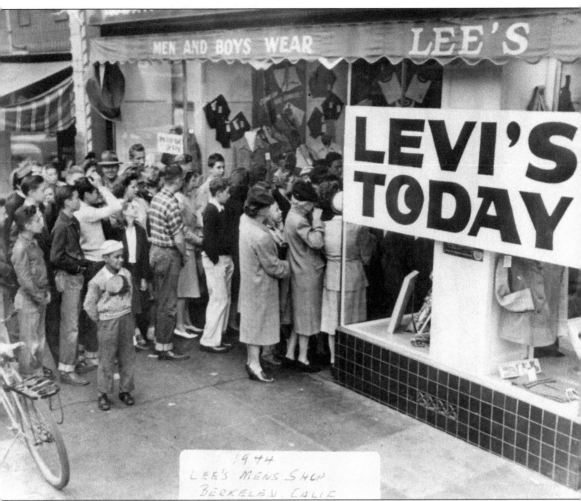

During World War II, the rationing of fabric and thread meant that LS&CO. could not produce their usual quantity of overalls, jackets, and shirts. After the war was over, it took awhile for production to get back up to speed, but once it did, when stores received their shipments, the line of consumers ran out the door. LS&CO. received many thank you letters from retailers, praising the company's efforts to help them get the product they needed during wartime.

By the late 1940s, LS&CO. had expanded its distribution from the West all the way to the Eastern states. For the first time, advertisements placed in newspapers and in stores featured the son of the family in the classroom and walking across campus instead of the working dad. Aimed at the new, suburban families and the young men going to college on the GI bill, it was nevertheless hard to convince Easterners that denim was appropriate for the high school or college boy.

LS&CO. created a few Western-themed pamphlets as gifts with purchase in the 1930s, such as this booklet of cowboy limericks, and these became more elaborate as the company moved into the war years and the 1950s. The series of "Western Lore" brochures debuted in the mid-1940s, featuring titles that always started with the phrase, "Levi's Round-Up Of," and covered topics such as western sheriffs, western horse lore, and western guns. Written by or in conjunction with well-known authors, these were designed to reinforce the links between the company, its famous products, and the still-fascinating American West.

For the first 90 years or so of LS&CO.'s history, the line "Since 1853" could be found on company letterhead and in catalogs, referring, of course, to the company's founding date. However, sometime around World War II, the line was changed to "Since 1850," and this date was cemented into company and popular culture via the increased advertising of the postwar years. In 1950, the company celebrated its "centennial." Held at the factory on Valencia Street, with luminaries such as California governor Earl Warren and San Francisco mayor Elmer Robinson in attendance, "1850" was considered the company's birth date until the early 1990s, when the LS&CO. Archives staff researched this discrepancy and were able to prove that 1853 was the true founding date. How this happened is still a mystery. Typographical errors in 19th-century newspaper articles are one explanation; another is a well-meaning decision to celebrate the company's centennial the same year as the state of California. However it happened, the official and accurate founding date of 1853 now graces all the company's printed and online materials. Pictured here from left to right are Daniel Koshland, Earl Warren, Elmer Robinson, and Walter Haas.

The Dude Ranch Duds line of the 1930s was renamed Western Wear by the end of the 1950s. Cowboy shirts in an array of patterned cotton fabrics replaced the rayon satin rodeo shirts of the 1930s and were meant to reflect the kind of clothing worn on popular television western series such as *Gunsmoke* and *Have Gun Will Travel*. There were also classic denim shirts for men and California Ranch Pants for women, slim-fitting slacks with Western detailing.

Sunscreens, which had been around since the 1930s, were originally designed to be used in the window of a Levi's retailer to both advertise the products and to keep the sun from fading whatever items were displayed there. The first sunscreen had the Two Horse logo and the phrase "Levi Strauss Overalls." By the 1950s, they featured elaborately painted cowboys and cowgirls with various advertising slogans and were displayed on walls rather than in windows. This version dates to the early 1950s.

A "Coropix" was a sort of proto-poster, created in the early 1950s as a display piece for Levi's retailers. There were two kinds of Coropix: one featured cowboys in goofy, comic situations, and the other had artwork of a more classic kind, with roundups, rodeos, etc. The designs were silk-screened onto corrugated cardboard, which allowed the scenes to be rolled for shipping. When unrolled, the Coropix could be pinned to a wall or framed once the excess corrugated board was cut off on either side of the image. Coropix were also used to help advertise special promotions, such as dude ranch vacations via Trans World Airlines.

LEVI'S ®
AMERICA'S FINEST OVERALL   SINCE 1850

This is the Saddleman, one of the company's most familiar symbols and trademarks. The Saddleman has been used in a variety of forms over the years: on woven labels in Western shirts, printed on brochures, printed on stationery for company events, woven as an emblem on polo shirts, and silk-screened onto T-shirts. This is a 3-foot-high plaster statue created in the early 1950s as in-store advertising for Levi's retailers.

The American family made its first appearance on Levi's advertising in the early 1950s. Young boys and their dads played on counter cards and in newspaper advertisements, where before they had been only working. Girls, however, would have to wait until the 1960s before they would be seen in jeans. During this decade, the word "overalls" was slowly being replaced in American culture with the word "jeans," thanks to the teenager. It is not clear why kids called the pants "jeans" (a word that dates to the 19th century and referred to pants made of a twill fabric called "jean"). It may have something to do with the way teenagers appropriated denim in the 1950s and the fact that "overalls" represented denim's past and that of their parents.

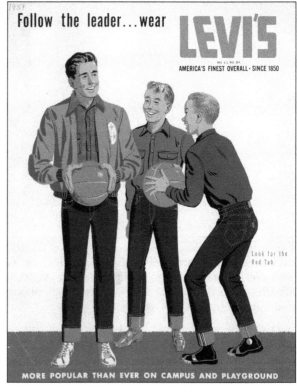

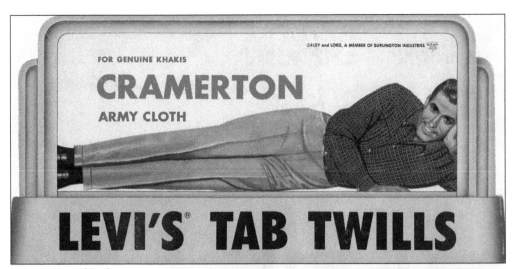

For Genuine Khakis

CRAMERTON
ARMY CLOTH

GALEY and LORD, A MEMBER OF BURLINGTON INDUSTRIES

LEVI'S® TAB TWILLS

Tab Twills and Lighter Blues were two other entries into the family-wear lineup of the 1950s. Tab Twills were khakis made of Cramerton Army cloth, the same cotton khaki fabric used by the U.S. military for uniforms. They were worn by workingmen, such as service-station attendants and repairmen, as well as college students. Young men who were not old enough to go to World War II wore khakis to emulate their older brothers, as khakis were often part of a soldier's uniform. Returning soldiers kept up with khakis as they went to college on the GI Bill. Lighter Blues, pants and jackets made of lightweight, light blue cotton, were the weekend wear for the American family.

BEYOND COMPARE FOR LEISURE WEAR

LEVI'S *Lighter Blues*

In response to the interest in denim as playwear, LS&CO. created the Denim Family line in the early 1950s. There was something for everyone in this line, which was made of sturdy but lightweight denim with subtle Western accents. It was well advertised in stores via counter cards and in newspapers and magazines. This reflected a change in attitude toward denim, which was now being seen as a fabric for leisure as well as labor. Trade magazines of the period make this very clear; in 1956, a writer for *American Fabrics* said that denim is in an "entirely new clothing category: it used to be work clothes, but now it's work 'n play clothes."

During the 1950s, LS&CO. made its first international forays, both in philanthropy and in business. During the Korean War, the company worked with the American Friends Service Committee to distribute jeans to refugees in Korea. In 1959, LS&CO. participated in a trade fair in Moscow, complete with displays of jeans and local "cowboy" singers.

Singer Bing Crosby was a faithful wearer of Levi's jeans and was once refused a room in a Vancouver hotel because he was wearing denim. LS&CO. heard about this and made him a denim tuxedo jacket, which was presented to him at the 1951 Silver State Stampede in Elko, Nevada, where he was honorary mayor. The company made replicas of the jacket for displays and a number of them are now in the LS&CO. Archives.

Spikes were launched in 1958—polished cotton slacks for men and boys in the colors of orange, lemon, and lime Jell-O brand gelatin. To advertise the product, and its color scheme, LS&CO. sent boxes of Jell-O to its retailers. The brightly colored pants were unfortunately ahead of their time, and Spikes did not go over well with either retailers or consumers.

Lady Levi's, which debuted in 1934, remained an important part of the Western Wear line through the 1950s. They were always considered leisure wear thanks to their dude ranch origins, and this continued to be reflected in in-store advertising in the 1950s. The "Right for Leisure" slogan echoed the "Right for School" advertising aimed at the young man of the family.

By the mid-1950s, LS&CO. was making men's and women's clothing under the Casuals label. In 1955, the women's Casuals line was so extensive it was given its own catalog, which was filled with the skirts, blouses, and "pedal pushers," popular in films and in suburban backyards. The clothes were heavily advertised in magazines such as *Glamour*, *Mademoiselle*, and *Seventeen*.

The American cowboy and the West have fascinated cultures outside of the United States for decades. In the 1950s, two European groups got together regularly to reenact scenes from American history and spend a few hours as cowboys. Pictured here are images from the Cowboy Club, Munich (founded in 1913), and the French Corral of the Westerners (founded in 1944 and later becoming Westerners International in 1959). (Photographs by Charles J. Belden.)

As the business grew in the 1950s, so did the company's presence in the windows of its retailers. Both the Western clothing and the casual wear took up a lot of well-designed real estate in stores both large and small. This display was at Cave and Walker in Tulare, California.

May Company
Los Angeles, Cal

Having casual playwear from Levi's in a store window was a big draw for retailers. This display graced the windows of the May Company in Los Angeles.

Six

PEACE, LOVE, AND BELL-BOTTOMS

As the 1960s dawned, LS&CO. focused its product design and advertising efforts toward a powerful new consumer: the teenager. Moving beyond denim, the company offered jean-styled pants for guys in twill and corduroy and slacks made of exciting new synthetics such as Avril rayon and Fortrel polyester. For girls, there were stretch jeans and striped, flowered, and otherwise-decorated casual pants.

Although the teenagers pictured in company catalogs were of the "clean cut" variety, the company was very aware of the ways that youth culture expressed itself. LS&CO. ran its first television advertisements in 1966 and in 1967 hired Jefferson Airplane to record radio commercials. These were recorded onto vinyl discs and given to salesmen to present to their retail customers to be run on local radio stations. When the poster came into vogue, LS&CO. hired famous artists such as Stanley Mouse, Victor Moscoso, and Bruce Wolfe to create memorable artwork to help market its products.

In 1968, LS&CO. created the Community Affairs Department, and two years later, the first of its Community Involvement Teams began volunteering in California communities, with the blessing and financial support of the company.

Global expansion was formalized in 1965 with the creation of the International Division, and by the late 1970s, there were LS&CO. affiliate offices throughout Europe and in Japan, Australia, and Canada. In order to help finance such expansion, LS&CO. went public for the first time in its history in 1971. Three years later, the corporate headquarters were relocated to the new Embarcadero Center, a little further north on Battery Street.

Leisure suits vied with decorated denim as fashion statements in the mid-1970s. LS&CO. launched the Levi's Denim Art Contest in 1973, a year after introducing the Panatela line of fashion slacks, tops, and suits. The company also clothed the American team at the 1980 Winter Olympics in Lake Placid, New York, and two years later moved into Levi's Plaza, world headquarters for the corporation, where it is still located today.

Walter Haas Jr. (1916–1995) came into the family business in 1939 and took over the presidency from Daniel Koshland in 1958. He brought a bright new generation of young leaders into the corporation and strengthened the company's commitment to social responsibility, especially in the area of racial integration in plant communities. After joining President Johnson's National Alliance of Businessmen, he created the Community Affairs Department and championed the first employee Community Involvement Teams, one of the company's bedrock programs of community service, going strong nearly 40 years later.

In 1960, LS&CO. decided to open a factory in Blackstone, Virginia, and encountered resistance to its plan to create a racially integrated facility, as government mandates on racial desegregation were a few years away. Vowing to take its jobs and go elsewhere unless the plant was allowed to integrate, city officials eventually relented.

In-store advertising in the 1960s not only continued to feature teenagers and college students, it also emphasized new styles and fabrics.

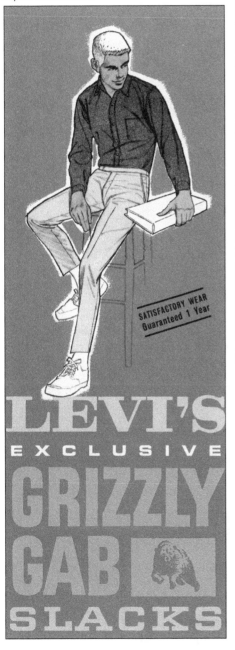

In the early 1960s, LS&CO. introduced its first preshrunk 501 jean, a new concept for old-timers who were used to buying their jeans a few inches too big to allow for the specially loomed fabric to shrink to fit them.

White Levi's started life as Slim Fits, pants in the five-pocket jean style made of either twill or corduroy. Because the pants were not blue, kids started to call them White Levi's, and the company eventually adopted the name.

LS&CO. sponsored dozens of promotions aimed at the interests of teenagers during the 1960s. This in-store advertisement for the "Donut 'n Dunk Hoedown" from around 1964 is typical; a space was left on the cardboard counter card for each individual store to use to write up the details of the promotion (presumably when the donuts would be served). Other promotions offered teens the opportunity to win a Kay brand guitar, a GE stereo, a Revell Grand Turismo racing set, or the Levi's Beach Buggy.

The popularity of foreign films was reflected in advertising for 1961: catalogs and display advertisements invoked movies such as *La Dolce Vita* and *Roman Holiday* in their design.

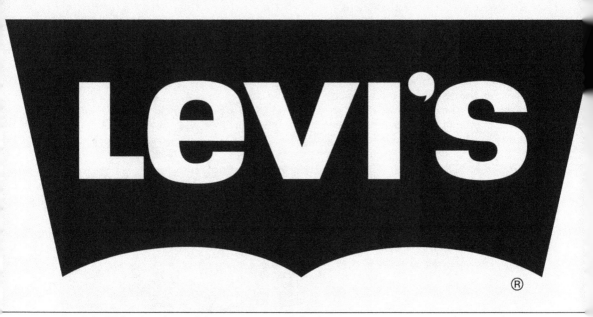

In 1967, Walter Landor and Associates created the famous Levi Strauss & Co. housemark. Previous corporate logos featured the word LEVI'S in all capital letters, but Walter Landor changed that when he put the word inside the "batwing" design, which mirrored the Arcuate stitching design on the back pocket of the jeans. He said the corporate identity should use the founder's name properly, with a capital "L" only. The design was created in red, the color of the signature Tab on the right back pocket.

When the red Tab was first used in 1936, it had the word LEVI'S woven in all capital letters. In 1971, the company decided to change the design to conform to the new housemark design—Levi's. When "vintage" Levi's jeans became a hot collectible in the late 1980s, the Tab's design became the dividing line between what was valuable and what was not. "Big E" (vintage) and "little e" (not vintage) Tabs are still the yardsticks by which collectible Levi's jeans are judged.

After the International Division was created in 1965, offices and factories opened at a steady rate all over the globe. These images date to the early 1960s when Levi's products were first being shown to dazzled international consumers at the Zurich City Fair (above) and at a shop in Tokyo (right).

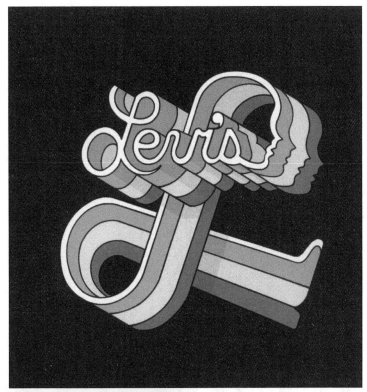

The women's clothing division was organized in 1968 and given the name Levi's for Gals. Its cheerful logo graced the labels of pants and shirts until the late 1970s, when the name was changed to Womenswear. In Europe, the name was Miss Levi's, with a product line similar to the stylish looks of Levi's For Gals. This LFG T-shirt from the early 1970s evoked the company's Western past.

San Francisco was the epicenter of 1960s counterculture, and some of its sensibility made its way into LS&CO.'s advertising during that decade. This advertisement for Bravo Levi's invoked rock concert posters in its design and the sea of young people is, of course, Woodstock.

Peter Haas Sr. (1918–2005) joined LS&CO. in 1945 and succeeded his brother as president in 1970. His interest in engineering led to his work with the manufacturing end of the business at the company's San Francisco plant, and this sparked his lifelong passion for and commitment to improving the lives of factory employees. Under his leadership, the company expanded internationally and went public for the first time in its history, while never losing sight of the concept of profits with principles.

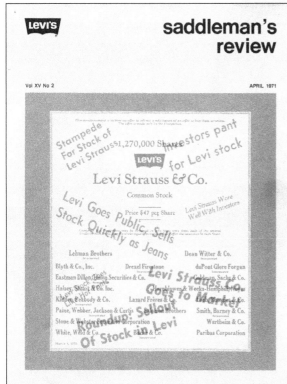

On March 3, 1971, Levi Strauss & Co. became a public corporation and took the unusual step of including a statement about social responsibility in its prospectus: "The Company's social responsibilities have for many years been a matter of strong conviction on the part of its management. Well before legal requirements were imposed, the Company was an 'equal opportunity employer.'" The company newsletter, *Saddleman's Review*, announced the IPO in its April 1971 issue.

SADDLEMAN'S REVIEW

Volume 17   Number 2
Fall 1973

Social Responsibility

"No corporation can prosper fully or long in a society frustrated by social ills and upheaval." This quote from Walter Haas Jr. typifies the consistent thread of good corporate citizenship that has been woven into LS&CO.'s culture since Levi himself ran the business. In 1973, the company devoted a full issue of the *Saddleman's Review* to its charitable efforts all over the United States. Articles about the company's heritage in social responsibility were printed along with stories of specific programs, punctuated with quotes from managers about the importance of balancing business and corporate compassion. The issue concludes with a number of management quotes, including this one from Peter Haas Sr.: "Certain objectives must be companywide: to be good citizens in the community, to follow understanding and progressive personnel practices, to recognize the dignity of the individual employee, to maintain the corporate integrity in every sense of the word."

After more than 60 years at 98 Battery Street, LS&CO. found that it needed more space for its corporate headquarters. In 1974, the company moved into Two Embarcadero Center, a newly constructed high-rise retail and office complex just a little further up Battery Street, but it was still in the same neighborhood where Levi Strauss had set up shop more than a century earlier.

The company's first boot-cut jean, created in 1969, was given the name of one of its favorite trademarks: Saddleman. In 1973, a postcard folder went out to retailers that featured examples of the Saddleman boot jean's newest fabrics on one side and historic images evoking the Western flavor of the pants on the other.

Embroidered, studded, sequined, painted: the craze for decorating denims inspired LS&CO. to announce the Levi's Denim Art Contest in 1973. This poster was placed in stores where Levi's products were sold, and it invited consumers to decorate their Levi's jeans, jackets, or shirts and send in slides of their work. The top 25 winners and the 24 honorable mentions were chosen in 1974 by a star-studded panel, including designer Rudi Gernreich, photographer Imogen Cunningham, writer and artist Alicia Bay Laurel, and other designers, critics, and curators from the San Francisco Bay Area. The winning pieces went on tour to American folk art museums and a few of them made their way to the LS&CO. Archives. The winners and honorable mentions were featured in a book called *Levi's Denim Art Contest*, published by rock photographer Baron Wolman.

One of the winning pieces from the Levi's Denim Art Contest, this oversized pair artistically depicts the issues and personalities of the 1973 Watergate hearings.

In the 1970s, LS&CO. offered consumers both denim and polyester in the newest styles, thanks to the popularity of "fashion" jeans in the "Me Decade." The company's first bell-bottom came along in 1969, initially in denim and then in blends of every fabric imaginable. In 1972, the Panatela line was created, offering dressier polyester products in the colors of the day. Panatela eventually became an entire menswear division, offering slacks and tops with names like Wildfire and David Hunter.

During the 1970s, American Motors Corporation offered "fashion" packages for its various models, including a Gucci Hornet and a Pierre Cardin Javelin. Both the Gremlin and the Jeep came in Levi's editions, complete with denim seats with copper buttons and the red "batwing" logo near the front wheel wells. The LS&CO. Archives owns a blue 1974 Levi's-edition Gremlin.

LS&CO. was famous for its illustrated posters in the 1970s and early 1980s and for hiring some of the most talented artists in the business. Victor Moscoso, Alton Kelly/Stanley Mouse, and Bruce Wolfe, among others, all created artwork that expressed both the essence of the Levi's brand and the sensibility of the period in which they were created. Here Bruce Wolfe's animals cavort in Panatela leisure suits. (Courtesy Bruce Wolfe, artist.)

LS&CO. clothed the American team at the 1980 Winter Olympics and planned to do the same for the Summer Olympics in Moscow, but the United States' boycott kept the athletes at home. Instead, LS&CO. outfitted all 550 athletes for a five-day celebration in Washington honoring the team. The company received six tickets for a White House dinner. Instead of passing them out to executives, chairman Walter Haas put the names of all U.S. employees into a hat and chose six people to attend the event. The winners went to the White House and met the athletes and Pres. Jimmy Carter.

WINTER PARADE

levi's

QUALITY NEVER GOES OUT OF STYLE.

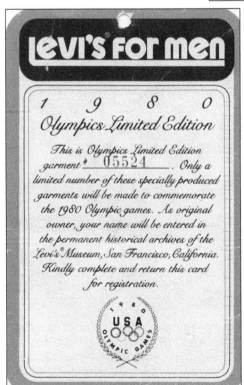

Despite the boycotted games in the summer of 1980, LS&CO. offered limited edition promotional pairs of jeans and gave consumers the opportunity to register their pair with the company in commemoration of the Olympics.

Bob Grohman became LS&CO.'s first non-family president and CEO in 1981. He joined LS&CO. in 1974, working initially to reorganize the European Division. He was head of the International Division and chief operating officer before leading LS&CO. He retired in 1984.

In 1979, ground was broken for LS&CO.'s new headquarters. By April 1982, a vacant lot on Battery Street at the Embarcadero had been transformed into Levi's Plaza, where world headquarters are still located today. San Francisco mayor Dianne Feinstein presided at the opening, and *San Francisco Chronicle* architecture critic Allen Temko described the plaza as "a social, economic, and taken in the broadest sense, environmental triumph."

Seven

150 YEARS . . . AND COUNTING

For Levi Strauss & Co., the 1980s were about being new. The company had a new CEO, Bob Haas; new television commercials that had everyone looking at the company's flagship product, the 501 jeans, in a completely different way; and a new world headquarters, Levi's Plaza, the physical expression of the company's unique culture.

In the following decade, the company continued and expanded the reach of its corporate citizenship. LS&CO. was the first major corporation to talk about the threat of HIV/AIDS in the workplace and to put its foundation's resources toward education and prevention. The company's Global Sourcing Guidelines of the early 1990s made workers rights another priority and led to similar codes being enacted at other firms.

Changes in the competitive environment of the 1990s required LS&CO. to transform the way it did business as the 21st century approached. The global popularity of jeans, the accessibility of high-quality denim, and a different generation of jeans lovers created opportunities for entrepreneurs—not unlike Levi Strauss himself—to start up new brands. The company therefore shifted its focus from owner and operated manufacturing to consumer-focused design innovation and marketing in order to be more agile in bringing new styles quickly to market.

The millennium itself began with good news: *Time* magazine named the 501 jean the fashion item of the 20th century, beating out the miniskirt and the little black dress. During celebrations to mark Levi's 150th anniversary, renewed interest in the company's merchandise came about via product innovations in the Levi's and Dockers brands and through the launch of the Levi Strauss Signature brand.

Today Levi Strauss & Co. remains the world's largest jeanswear purveyor and is a global leader in casual apparel, selling its products in more than 110 countries around the globe. LS&CO. has come a long way since its namesake first stepped off a steamship and into San Francisco history more than 150 years ago. It has stayed true to the founder's ideals even as it continues to meet the needs of the global consumer of the 21st century.

Bob Haas, son of Walter Haas Jr., joined LS&CO. in 1973 and became CEO in 1984, the beginning of an unprecedented period of growth and prosperity for the company. He took the company private in 1985 via a now-legendary leveraged buyout and oversaw the creation of the Dockers brand. Under his leadership, LS&CO. pioneered HIV/AIDS awareness and education programs that are the benchmark for those adopted by other corporations. In 1991, LS&CO. pioneered the first manufacturing code of conduct and the following year became the first Fortune 500 company to extend medical benefits to employees' domestic partners. Bob has also received national recognition for his leadership in corporate philanthropy and for launching Project Change, a program designed to combat institutional racism. Bob is chairman of the company's board of directors.

LS&CO. clothed every American associated with the 1984 Summer Olympics in Los Angeles, from athletes to vendors. This is the velour warm-up suit worn by the athletes, an item that shows up regularly on eBay.

Levi's® U.S.A. Olympic warm-up in rich panne velour.

During the 1984 Summer Olympics in Los Angeles, LS&CO. launched the "501 Blues" advertising campaign. The commercials featured something new in the world of television advertisements—young people just doing their thing wearing their Levi's jeans, accompanied by bluesy music and filmed with the now-familiar "shaky camera" technique. They were a huge hit and helped contribute to the popularity of the jeans and the brand.

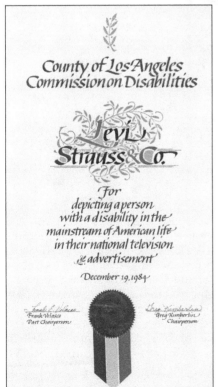

County of Los Angeles
Commission on Disabilities

Levi
Strauss & Co.

For
depicting a person
with a disability in the
mainstream of American life
in their national television
advertisement

December 19, 1984

Frank Velasco
Past Chairperson

Greg Kimberlin
Chairperson

One of the "501 Blues" television advertisements featured a young man in a wheelchair, wearing his Levi's jeans, moving to the music with his friends. The New York State Office of Advocates for the Disabled awarded LS&CO. its Governor's Committee Media/Advertising Award for the commercial's positive portrayal of a disabled person.

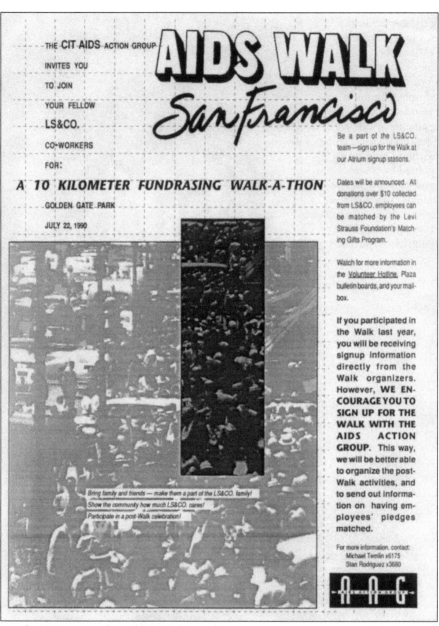

In the early 1980s, a number of LS&CO. employees went to management with their concerns about a new disease that was ravaging the gay population: AIDS. While other companies ignored the epidemic, LS&CO. faced this growing threat by openly discussing the disease, its causes, and helping alleviate employee fears. In 1982, the Levi Strauss Foundation, the first corporate foundation to address the epidemic, made its first matching gifts to the Kaposi Sarcoma Clinic at San Francisco General Hospital. Comprehensive education and health services for employees and their families were developed the following year. LS&CO. has a dominant presence at the AIDS Walk each year, and the Levi Strauss Foundation has contributed more than $37 million to HIV/AIDS services in more than 40 countries. These progressive practices have earned LS&CO. numerous awards over the years, including the 2007 Leadership Award from the San Francisco AIDS Foundation.

Khakis have been a quiet presence throughout LS&CO.'s history. While denim has dominated, the company started making khaki pants and other clothing as early as 1905. In 1986, LS&CO. introduced Dockers khakis to the American market, though the brand has international origins. In 1984, Levi's Argentina developed a line of "nautically inspired" fashion jeans, which were given the name "Dockers," and Levi Strauss Japan used the name for some casual pants they introduced in 1985—Docker Pants. The following year, noting that the baby-boomer male needed a pair of pants that would fill the space between his jeans and his three-piece suit, LS&CO. launched Dockers. The brand's innovative television commercials were both popular and parodied on prime-time television.

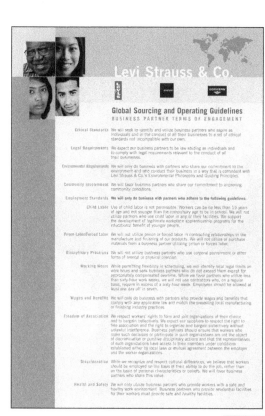

In the late 1980s, employees began to raise concerns about the working conditions of the company's overseas factory workers. This led LS&CO. to create a supplier code of conduct in 1991 that ensured all individuals making its products would be treated with dignity and work in a safe and healthy environment. LS&CO. was the first multinational apparel company to establish a comprehensive set of principles for manufacturing. Called the Global Sourcing and Operating Guidelines, it was initially treated with skepticism, but today codes of conduct are an apparel-industry norm and are rapidly being adopted by companies in other industries.

After nearly 150 years of being a wholesale business exclusively, LS&CO. opened its first retail store in 1983, in Spain. The first U.S. stores opened in 1991. At this writing, LS&CO. has 138 company-operated stores in 18 countries. Pictured here are Levi's stores in Europe and Asia.

AT HOME ON THE RANGE WITH LEVI'S

YOUR FAVORITE SONGS

With drawings by the Cowboy Artist

LEE M. RICE

Music has long been associated with the Levi's brand and its products. In the 1930s, the company printed a brochure of traditional cowboy songs as a gift with purchase, which included the full lyrics of songs like "The Cowboy's Lament." In 1949, the film *Deputy Marshal* featured a song titled "Levi's, Plaid Shirt and Spurs." In the 1960s, garments aimed at teenagers also showed up in popular songs. The Majorettes recorded a tune called "White Levi's" in 1964, and in 1967, Jefferson Airplane recorded a number of radio advertisements about White Levi's and Stretch Levi's. Bruce Springsteen wore 501 jeans on the cover of the classic *Born in the U.S.A.* album. In 1995, Levi Strauss Japan sponsored the Tokyo venue for the Rolling Stones' Voodoo Lounge tour and the group signed a pair of jeans and a jacket, which are now in the LS&CO. Archives. The company has also sponsored a number of musicians and their tours over the years, including Christina Aguilera and 'NSync.

In 1993, LS&CO. held the "Send Them Home Search," a contest to find the oldest pair of Levi's jeans owned by a consumer. The winning pair, found by a college student in the garbage dump of a mining town near Gold Hill, Nevada, dated to the late 1920s. The back pocket was customized by its original owner with a flap and button from a pair of khaki pants. (Photograph by Hangauer/Kissinger.)

In the 1990s, LS&CO. decided to tap into the craze for collecting "vintage" Levi's jeans and created a line of authentic reproductions of jeans and other clothing from the LS&CO. Archives. In 1996, Levi's Vintage Clothing was launched, and collections of archival clothing are made for the North America, Europe, and Asia regions each year.

Phil Marineau became CEO of Levi Strauss & Co. in 1999. Formerly the president and CEO of Pepsi-Cola North America, Phil also spent 23 years with Quaker Oats. During his tenure at LS&CO., he led the company through a successful business turnaround, oversaw the launch of the Levi Strauss Signature® brand, improved the company's profitability, and launched Community Day worldwide.

Located on historic Union Square, the 24,000-square-foot Levi's store in San Francisco opened in 1999, just across Stockton Street from where Levi Strauss lived from 1863 to 1864.

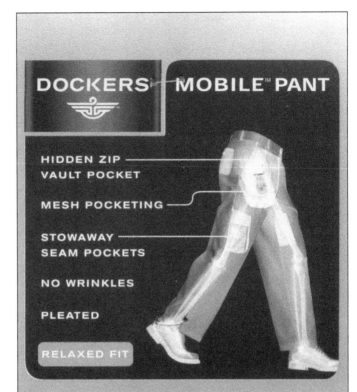

The Dockers San Francisco brand charged into the 21st century with innovative products and technologies that responded to the needs of the modern consumer. In 2001, it introduced the Dockers Mobile Pant, which has invisible pockets for the discreet storage of high-tech gadgetry. Next came the Go Khaki with Stain Defender, which uses nanotechnology to defend against liquid spills.

In 2003, LS&CO. celebrated the 150th anniversary of the company's founding and the 130th anniversary of the invention of the blue jean. To celebrate these dual occasions, the lobby of world headquarters in San Francisco was transformed into the Visitors Center, with exhibits about the history of the company, its clothing, advertising, corporate citizenship, and nearly a century of correspondence with consumers. Display cases with historic garments went on tour throughout the United States, Europe, and Asia and helped tell the company's story during the summer and early fall of 2003. In summer 2007, a new exhibition about the LS&CO. Archives—The Vault—opened in the Visitors Center.

LEVI STRAUSS
Signature®

While LS&CO. was celebrating its 150th anniversary in 2003, a new brand was being launched: Levi Strauss Signature, designed for consumers who shop at mass-channel retail stores. The new brand is, in many ways, a return to the company's roots, giving value-oriented consumers access to products from a company with a heritage of high-quality jeanswear.

California State Assembly

Certificate Of

Recognition

PRESENTED TO:

Levi Strauss & Co.

IN HONOR OF:

Being Named To The
AIDS Walk San Francisco 2002 Gold Team

November 22, 2001

Kevin Shelley

MEMBER OF THE ASSEMBLY

12th ASSEMBLY DISTRICT
CALIFORNIA STATE LEGISLATURE

Levi Strauss & Co. has received dozens of awards and acknowledgements over the last half-century. This recognition comes for the work of the Levi Strauss Foundation, the company's ethical business practices, LS&CO.'s storied heritage, and the Haas family's commitment to volunteerism and community service.

Certificate of Honor

BOARD OF SUPERVISORS
City and County of San Francisco

The Board of Supervisors of the City and County of San Francisco hereby issues, and authorizes the execution of, this Certificate of Honor in appreciative public recognition of distinction and merit for outstanding service to a significant portion of the people of the City and County of San Francisco by:

THE LEVI STRAUSS FOUNDATION

In appreciation of your 15 years of support for Project Open Hand and the almost $300,000 in funding grants you have provided. In recognition of your vital role as one of Project Open Hand's first corporate supporters in the early days of the HIV/AIDS epidemic. And honoring your worldwide philanthropic leadership and your dedication to reflecting the voices of communities where Levi Strauss & Company does business, such as San Francisco. The Board of Supervisors of the City and County of San Francisco extends to you its highest commendation.

Supervisor Bevan Dufty
Member, San Francisco Board of Supervisors
March 13th, 2003

John Anderson became president and CEO of Levi Strauss & Co. in November 2006. He joined Levi Strauss & Co. in 1979 and has worked around the world in positions such as general manager of Levi Strauss Canada, interim president of Levi Strauss Europe, and, most recently, president of the Asia Pacific Division, where he helped double sales for the region and increased the presence of all three of the company's brands. A native of Australia, John is also LS&CO.'s first CEO to come from outside the United States.

As part of its commitment to employee volunteerism, LS&CO. holds Community Day each year. Teams of employees go to agencies throughout San Francisco and the Bay Area performing needed services such as painting walls, removing graffiti, clearing brush, or packing boxes.

Levi's Plaza, world headquarters of Levi Strauss & Co. in San Francisco, is just a few short blocks from

the spot where Levi Strauss began his business in 1853. (Photograph by Hangauer/Kissinger.)

Visit us at
arcadiapublishing.com

CPSIA information can be obtained
at www.ICGtesting.com
Printed in the USA
LVHW100558301220
675396LV00013B/953